# STRATHCONON

## The History and Archaeology of a Northeast Highland Glen

By Meryl Marshall

©North of Scotland Archaeological Society

website www.nosas.co.uk

Printed by A4 Design & Print Ltd, Inverness

Published, June 2011, by the North of Scotland Archaeological Society

ISBN No 978-0-9568786-0-1

# Forward

When the Scotland's Rural Past project was being conceived in the early 2000s, amongst the many aims of those planning it was that the surveys undertaken by the local volunteers who came together to undertake the work would throw some light on what was hitherto a much-neglected and scarcely understood period in our nation's history. It was hoped that surveys could be drawn together to provide a clearer picture of the surviving evidence for 18th to 20th century rural settlement and on its much earlier origins. Perhaps no group took these hopes and aims more to heart than the enthusiastic volunteers who took on the ambitious project of surveying the whole of the upper reaches of Strathconon, a glen into which few archaeologists had trodden. The result is this magnificent volume, where history, archaeology, architecture and ethnography are drawn together into a fascinating overview of the glen, its landscape, environment, and its people. It is to be hoped that others will find inspiration and encouragement in it to carry on with the task of surveying and researching the still undiscovered heritage locked in Scotland's rural landscape.

Richard Oram, Professor of Medieval and Environmental History, University of Stirling, Chair SRP External Management Board

# and from NOSAS

This is NOSAS's second book. Last time Meryl covered a slightly smaller area, Glen Feshie, with a different slant, this time the task of surveying and recording the archaeology of Strathconon took 3 years. The organisational skills of gathering NOSAS volunteers, taking them out to collect the raw data and then processing it for the national and local records cannot be underestimated. Not only did Meryl achieve this, she also involved the local community with a variety of events and undertook extensive research in the National Archives of Scotland. In producing this book she has drawn together all these strands to give us the full story of a Highland strath during a time of massive change. From the end of the 18th century when whisky was a high value, albeit illicit, product through the privations of the 19th century and into the beginning of the 20th century, the life of the people is vividly brought to life. In producing this book we should also like to thank our funders for their generous assistance. We hope you enjoy the journey though Strathconon.

Anne Coombs – NOSAS Chairperson

# Enjoy Scotland's outdoors responsibly

Everyone has the right to be on most land and inland water providing they act responsibly. Your access rights and responsibilities are explained fully in the Scottish Outdoor Access Code.

Whether you're in the outdoors or managing the outdoors, the key things are to:

- **take responsibility for your own actions**
- **respect the interests of other people**
- **care for the environment.**

Visit **outdooraccess-scotland.com** or contact your local Scottish Natural Heritage office.

SCOTTISH **OUTDOOR ACCESS** CODE

**KNOW THE CODE BEFORE YOU GO**
**outdooraccess-scotland.com**

# Contents

Preface

1. Introduction      9

2. Placenames of Strathconon      15

3. The prehistoric period in Strathconon      19

4. The rise of Clan Mackenzie and the fall of the      23
   Earl of Seaforth, their chief

5. Strathconon and the Mackenzies in the      29
   sixteenth and seventeenth centuries

6. The history of Scatwell and the lower glen      39

7. The pre-improvement period –      41
   black cattle and the shieling system

8. Improvement and sheepfarming      53

9. Survival, migration and the fate of a large population      59

10. "Still-Life" in Strathconon – the story of illicit whisky production      77

11. The ecclesiastical background of Strathconon      87

12. New landlords and new initiatives -      93
    from sporting estates to hydroelectricity

13. The story of Finlay MacIver and his family      103

Bibliography

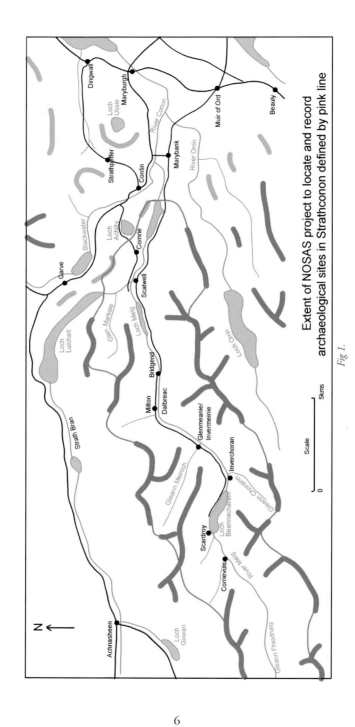

Fig 1.

Extent of NOSAS project to locate and record
archaeological sites in Strathconon defined by pink line

# Preface

In the Autumn of 2006 the North of Scotland Archaeological Society embarked on a project to identify, survey and record the archaeology of Strathconon, it was to be part of the Scotland's Rural Past Scheme which was a nationwide initiative aimed at encouraging amateur archaeologists to record the many rural settlements in the Scottish countryside. The area of Strathconon was an ambitious target and it took three years to complete, but by the end we had unearthed so much that was new and of interest that it was felt appropriate to make it available to everyone in the form of a publication. This book entirely complements Duncan Maclennan's previous work on Strathconon which gives an account of his time as a manager and employee of the landowner in the earlier part of last century. He gives us a view of the social history in the period from the year 1900; this book covers the history and archaeology of the period up until that time.

Our project involved many hours of fieldwork. We scoured the valley and tramped the hills looking for archaeological remains at all times of the year and in every kind of weather. We took details of the sites and on occasions drew plans and sketches. It was hard work and a labour of love but there were significant rewards, and at the end of the day it has been very satisfying to uncover the story of the glen.

Researching the history of the glen by delving into the documentary resources is an important part of a project such as this. Visits were made to the National Archive of Scotland (NAS) in Edinburgh and resulted in some useful information. Of particular note were the early 18th century rentals of the estate after it had been forfeited following the 1715 Uprising. A list of male inhabitants, between the ages of 15 and 60, compiled under settlement names and collected by the minister of Contin Parish in 1798 was also very useful. Aonghas MacCoinnich of the University of Strathclyde undertook some new documentary research into the period prior to 1700 for us. An abridged version of his essay "Strathconon, Scatwell and the Mackenzies in the written record, c.1463 – c.1700" is included as Chapter 5. The Highland Archive Centre in Inverness was visited and also the library; Old Parish Records (OPRs), census records of 1841 to 1901, evidence given to the Royal Commissions of 1883 (Napier Commission) and 1892 (Deer Commission) and newspapers with advertised "lets" going back to 1808 were all consulted. A number of secondary sources gave helpful information too, Iain Macdonald's book "Glencoe and Beyond – The Sheepfarming Years 1780-1830" for example, gave some details of the early sheepfarming tacks, and Dixon's "Gairloch" had a tale on cattle-thieving relevant to Scardroy. Old maps were essential to our research. The estate map of 1825[1] gave limited information whereas the plan of 1853[2] which depicted the populated area around Milltown, Dalbreac, Porin, Dalnacroich and Bridgend was much more detailed – it is an example of a "gentleman's map" and is likely to have been commissioned as much for its decorative purposes. As always the Roy map of c.1750 was helpful but only for the lower glen, and the First Edition Ordnance Survey map of 1881 (surveyed 1875) was useful. Inevitably the survival of documents is patchy and there are omissions in the historical records. It proved difficult, for example, to

[1] NAS RHP 2525
[2] NAS RHP 2521

find documents relating to the Scatwell estate prior to 1850 and documents for the Strathconon Estate in the 1820s and 1830s seem to be scanty in their survival.

The subject of the "clearances" is a controversial and, for Strathconon, an unavoidable topic. In writing about this I have tried not to pass an opinion but rather to present the facts of the situation in the glen, letting the reader make up his/her own mind about the events.

Copies of the full reports, produced following the completion of each phase of the project, are deposited with the Historic Environment Record (Highland Council), the National Monument Record of Scotland (Edinburgh), Historic Scotland, Dingwall Museum and Dingwall Library.

We would like to acknowledge the permission for access and co-operation of the landowners of the three estates of Strathconon, Scatwell and Scardroy. The help and assistance given to us by the keepers of these estates; Angus Cameron for Strathconon, Colin Hendry for Scardroy and Mike Watt for Scatwell was invaluable and encouraging. Our thanks are extended to Aonghas MacCoinnich for his interest and his essay and Michael Brander for permission to reproduce old photographs and maps. The involvement, interest and knowledge of the people of the glen was much appreciated and finally our thanks go to the Fairburn Windfarm Community Benefit Fund and the Highland Council Ward Discretionary Fund for their financial assistance towards producing this book.

# 1. Introduction

A road sign at Marybank, 6 miles west of Dingwall, announces "Welcome to Strathconon – Scenic glen for 17 miles, no through road to the west". The glen is long and beautiful, of that there is no doubt, and it has no through road today, but it has not always been that way; in previous days the glen was an important route between the east and the west coasts. Strathconon sees few visitors today, perhaps because there is no through road, but also perhaps because there are no mountains of any significance; the hills are, in the main, rounded, rolling and heathery with just 3 or 4 summits over 2,500 feet.

*Fig 2.* View across the wooded area of Scatwell towards Glenmarksie and Loch Luichart

The name Strathconon is something of a misnomer as, for the most part, the valley is occupied by the River Meig, the River Conon only joining it from Loch Luichart at Scatwell in the lower valley. Strathconon is a good example of a valley with a U-shaped profile, the flat valley floor with steep sides having been formed by the scouring action of glaciation. Loch Beannacharain in the upper valley is the only natural loch. Lochs Meig and Achonachie in the lower glen are man made and have been formed by dams for the purpose of creating electricity.

This book covers the archaeology and history of the glen from the Achonachie Dam westwards, an area that comprises the three estates of Strathconon, Scardroy and Scatwell; the smaller estate of Scardroy to the west was originally part of the Strathconon Estate. The lower part of the glen, around Scatwell and Loch Achonachie, has seen considerable development in recent times resulting in commercial forestry and hydro-schemes with their dams, power lines and realigned roads leaving their mark. The upper glen is more barren and mountainous, but the valley floor provides some good grazing ground as far west as Scardroy and Corrievuic. Most of the population, which numbers about 100 today, is in the central part of the glen at the settlements of Dalbreac, Milton, Dalnacroich, Porin and Bridgend, and the school and community hall which serve this community are located here. In former days there was also a grain mill, a smiddy and an inn.

From late medieval times until the early 19th century, Strathconon was a small but important part of the estates of Mackenzie of Kintail, chief of the Clan Mackenzie and later Earl of Seaforth. Rentals for the forfeited estate in 1717[1] indicate that the proportion of value of Strathconon and Strathbran (the adjacent glen to the north which was also Seaforth property) to the whole estate was less than 10%. Seaforth's vast estates included Brahan, his main residence, the Isle of Lewis, Kintail, Lochalsh and Lochcarron as well as Strathconon and Strathbran. Scatwell Estate has been separate from the rest of Strathconon from early days, having been granted by the Mackenzie chief to a younger son who had established one of the many Mackenzie cadet branches.

The surnames which predominated in Strathconon in the early rentals were MacRae and McLennan, clans based in the west that were fiercely loyal to Clan Mackenzie. There were many people too with the surname Macdonald, perhaps a legacy from a time when the glen was one of the major routes from the west and when the Macdonalds held the Earldom of Ross.

It is possible that Strathconon was used as a routeway even in prehistoric times, but it is not until medieval times that there is firm evidence in the documentary record of travellers in the glen. In 1411 Donald Macdonald, Lord of the Isles, in pursuit of his claim to the Earldom of Ross, journeyed from the west via Strathconon; he was intent

*Fig 3.* Upper Strathconon and the ruins of the keeper's cottage and byre at Corriefeol

[1] NAS E655-1-2

on taking Dingwall Castle and was successful in defeating a counter claim of the Munros and Mackenzies at the conflict of Blar n'Inich, near Strathpeffer

Donald Macdonald marched his force from the River Farrer and followed the route: Glen Ling, Glen Fiodaic, Strathconon and Contin (Cromartie, 1979).

Travelling in early times was difficult; not only was there the danger of becoming entangled in the inter-clan feuding or cattle thieving that was prevalent in these times, but there was also the hostile climate and terrain to contend with. One minister writing about the country at the end of the 18th century observed

The most inland parts (of the Highlands) are nothing but a vast group of dreadful mountains, with their summits piercing the clouds and divided only by deep and narrow valleys whose declivities are so rugged and steep as to be dangerous to travellers not furnished with guides.....Travelling it must be owned is difficult and disagreeable, there are no roads but such as the feet of men and cattle have made (Old Statistical Account, 1791).

The Roy map of 1750 marks a track through Strathconon, the only one from east to west in this part of Ross-shire; it would have been a bridle path for people on foot or horseback and quite unfit for wheeled vehicles. This track took a different line from the road today, staying on the south side of the river, crossing over to the north side at Inverchoran and taking a higher line along the north side of Loch Beannacharain to Scardroy. It then headed northwest and crossed a low pass to Loch Gowan, near Achnasheen. At Luib Gargan, near Loch Gowan, there was an inn where the host was John Macdonald, described as "vintner" on the 1798 list[2]. Parts of the old track are seen at Carnoch and Scardroy, and from Bridgend to Dalbreac the early track followed the line of the present estate road. A road from Luib Gargan to Carnoch was proposed in 1807, surveyed in 1835 and 1844[3] but does not seem to have been constructed until much later and even then was not surfaced for much of its length.

Osgood Mackenzie writes about his father travelling from Conon House to Gairloch in about 1800

A troop of men and some 30 ponies came from Gairloch, everything had to go west and I have heard that my father was carried to Gairloch on pony back in a kind of cradle when he was only a few weeks old. The plan was to start in the afternoon for the little inn at Scatwell at the foot of Strathconon as there was a road of a kind thus far, the old yellow coach carried the quality (ie the gentry) there before dark. There were several difficulties in those days. One was the crossing of the various fords over the rivers and the next was keeping dry all the precious things. Next morning the start was made at 6 o'clock right up Strathconon and across the high beallach into Strath Bran and on till Kenlochewe was reached (Mackenzie, 1921).

James Hogg, the Ettrick shepherd, was one who visited the glen in 1802 with a mind to taking a tack (Hogg, 1803) and Donald Sage passed this way in 1814

Leaving Attadale in the morning I breakfasted at Luibgargan, proceeded on foot down Strathconan and rested during the night at Garve (Sage, 1899).

[2] NAS GD46-17-80-200-0001
[3] NAS GD433-3-3-8

*Fig 4.* The bridge spanning the River Meig at Bridgend

By 1803 the road from Dingwall to Loch Carron, via Achnasheen and Strath Bran, seems to have been a popular alternative route and the construction of the turnpike road along this line in 1820 led to the Strathconon route gradually falling into disuse. A good road was however constructed in Strathconon in the 1830s, from Scatwell to Milton, and the bridge at Bridgend was constructed at this time. This bridge at NH 32257 54947 is still in use and has been listed by Historic Scotland. With the construction of the hydro-schemes parts of the road have been re-aligned and a further bridge at Balnault has been bypassed. At Bridgend the road on the south side of the river and the second bridge, over the Allt a'Bhogair, provided the original access to the Lodge and were probably constructed in the 1840s as part of the development of Dalbreac Lodge. The road from Milton westwards as far as Scardroy was not completed until 1852 and was constructed at the expense of the landowner of that time, James Maitland Balfour.

Travellers through the glen in early times may have stayed at one of the two inns in the glen. At Dalnacroich the inn is still in use as a dwelling house, and at Scatwell the inn is reported as being either on the site of the present lodge or at Curin. There were connecting routes from other glens to north and west; that from Scardroy has already been mentioned and that to the inn at Badinluchie, near Achanalt in Strathbran, headed north from Dalnacroich.

From early times the glen seems to have been extremely well populated. It was reported as one of the most congested areas in the Highlands and one writer in the 19th century refers to the "superabundant population"[4]. It was a pastoral community and, as in most parts of the Highlands, would have relied heavily on cattle in the years up to 1800. The archaeological remains in the glen provide a tantalizing glimpse into the lives of this

[4] NAS GD46-17-59-00003

population. The sites are not spectacular; this has not been a significant place in history, but what the archaeology lacks in quality and scale it makes up for in quantity. This is particularly the case in the upper glen where there has been less development and where the subsequent activity of sheep and cattle farming has led to the preservation of the low grassy footings of the buildings. In the lower glen many of the sites have been destroyed by forestry or inundated by water and, of those remaining, many are overgrown with bracken and heather making them difficult to find.

*Fig 5*. Aerial Photograph of Corriefeol and Corrievuic in Upper Strathconon
©Crown Copyright RCAHMS. Licensor www.rcahms.gov.uk

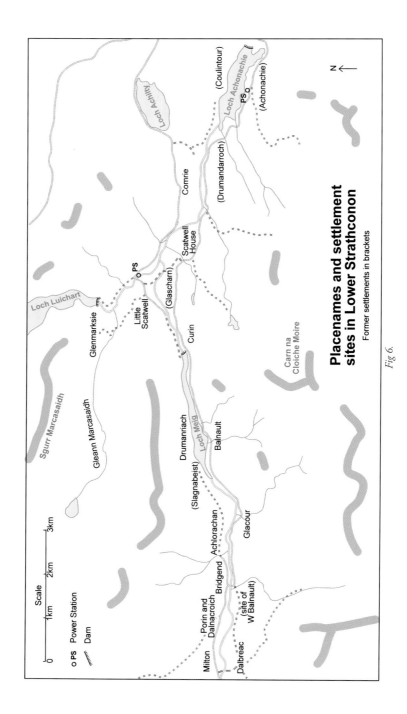

Scale

0 1km 2km 3km

o **PS** Power Station

⌢⌢⌢ Dam

Sgurr Marcasaidh

Gleann Marcasaidh

Loch Luichart

Glenmarksie

Little Scatwell

(Glascharn)

o **PS**

Scatwell House

Comrie

Loch Achilty

(Drumandarroch)

Loch Achonachie

**PS** o

(Coulintour)

(Achonachie)

Curin

Drumanriach

(Slagnabeist)

Loch Meig

Balnault

Carn na Cloiche Moire

Achlorachan

Glacour

Milton

Porin and Dalnacroich

Bridgend

(site of W Balnault)

Dalbreac

N ←

## Placenames and settlement sites in Lower Strathconon

Former settlements in brackets

*Fig 6.*

14

# 2. Placenames of Strathconon

Placename study can give information and important clues to the history and background of an area, but over the years spellings of the placenames may change, a name can be transferred to another location or a name may fall out of use. Placenames did not become consistent until the 1870s when the Ordnance Survey mapped the country and produced their first edition maps. In 1904 WJ Watson published *Placenames of Ross and Cromarty* and today his book still remains a useful reference (Watson, 1904).

The name Strathconon, which appears in 1479 as Strquhonane (Watson, 1904), is thought to mean the "valley of Connan", although who Connan was nobody seems to know. The source of the River Meig, which runs through Strathconon, is Glen Fhiodaig, sometimes known as Glen Uaig, either of which may have given the river its name.

The Exchequer Rolls of 1486 provide evidence of several settlements in Strathconon at that time; Kenloch Benquherane, Innerquhowran, Innermany and Meyn are mentioned (Munro and Munro, 1986). Kenloch Benquherane or Kinlochbeancharan in later documents means "head of the loch of the place of the peaks" in Gaelic; it is now known as Scardroy and the lodge, with its policies, occupies the site of the former township. Innerquhowran is now Inverchoran and Innermany is Invermeinie or Glenmeinie (on the current OS map), sometimes also known as Invervannie or Inverveinie. The placename Meyn, sometimes spelt as Meinn or Maine, is much more complicated and has fallen out of use over the years although it survives in Cladh Meinn, the old name for the burial ground at Porin, and perhaps also in Glen Meanich and its river. In rentals of 1726-28[1] the lands of "Meyne" comprise Balnault (which in these early days was on the south side of the river at the present Bridgend; later when the site we know of today as Balnault (East) was established it was known as West Balnault), Tornishiangain (location unknown), Dalnacroich, Pourin Easter, Pourin Wester, Knockdow (thought to be west of Dalbreac Lodge), Baillespoutan (thought to be present day Milton), Strathanmore, Mullich (location unknown), and Delbreck. Watson (1904) puts forward the suggestion that "meinn" means "ore" in Gaelic and that the term is usually applied where the water is coloured by the rust of oxidized iron. Reinforcing this connection with iron, Aonghas MacCoinnnich in Chapter 5 makes reference to documents connecting Strathconon with Kinlochewe, where it is known that the resource of iron was exploited in the late 16th Century (see also MacCoinnich, 2009).

Strathconon has many Gaelic placenames but also a few Norse placenames indicating that the Norse at least visited the glen in early medieval times even if they didn't settle. The name Scatwell has Norse origins and has been thought to mean a place for paying tribute or tax - "skat" meaning tax and "vollr", a field, but a further suggestion is that it derives from the Old Norse word "scat" meaning "the top of a tree" or "the furthest end of something" and the word "val" used for land which has been felled and cleared by burning (Crawford, 1995). Many of the Norse placenames in Ross-shire seem to be

[1] NAS E655-3-5, E655-3-4 and E655-3-2

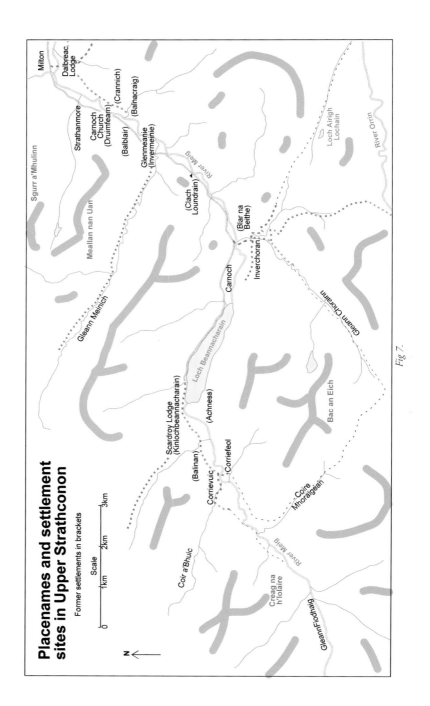

# Placenames and settlement sites in Upper Strathconon

Former settlements in brackets

Scale

0  1km  2km  3km

N ←

Milton
Dalbreac Lodge
Strathanmore
Carnoch Church (Druimfeàrn)
(Crannich)
(Balblair)
(Balnacraig)
Glenmeanie (Invermeinie)
Sgurr a'Mhulinn
Meallan nan Uan
(Clach Loundrain)
River Meig
(Blar na Beithe)
Inverchoran
Carnoch
Gleann Meinich
Loch Airigh Lochain
River Orrin
Gleann Chorainn
Loch Beannacharain
Scardroy Lodge (Kinlochbeannacharain)
(Achness)
Bac an Eich
(Balinan)
Corrievuic
Corriefeol
Coire Mhoraigean
Coir a'Bhuic
River Meig
Creag na h'Iolaire
Gleann Fiodhaig

Fig 7.

16

connected with trees and timber. Another Norse name in Strathconon found only in old documents is that of Eskatellis or Eskadale. It probably refers to the part of the glen which includes Loch Meig, Balnault, Drumanriach, Glacour, Druminbuie and Achlorachan. "Eskadale in Strathconon" appears in early 15th century charters and in the Exchequer Rolls but it has been lost over the centuries. The most recent reference to it is in a Seaforth rental of 1726[2]; under "Strathconin and Strathbren", tenants are named as in "one quarter of Eskadel" and "the other western quarter of Eskadell in Strathconan". Barbara Crawford puts forward the plausible suggestion that the first element means "askr" or "ash tree", and the second element "dal" or valley (Crawford 1995). The name, Eskadale is yet another placename which may refer to timber and, along with "Scatwell", may indicate that the glen was used by the Norse for its timber reserves. An Eskadale is still extant in Strathglass where it is an ancient religious site in the middle reaches of the glen; a similar location in Strathglass to this in Strathconon.

As with other glens in the Highlands, the placenames that predominate in Strathconon are Gaelic. One only has to look at the Ordnance Survey map to see how widespread they are. The names often give clues to the history of the place, Dalnacroich for instance provides evidence of a gallows; "there is a hillock called Cnoc na Croiche (meaning "hill of the cross") where malefactors are supposed to have been buried" (Watson, 1904) and Milton is the site of a mill and the burn, Allt Bail' a' Mhuilinn or "stream of the township of the mill", has provided water power for a series of mills. Carnoch, means "place of cairns" suggestive of stone clearance for cultivation and Scardroy or Sgaird Rhuadh is thought to mean "red scree" although a tale in Dixon's book (1886) suggests that it came about as a result of cattle being driven over rough ground so that their feet bled.

The names of features in the landscape can also give an indication of past activity. Loch Airigh Lochain, to the east of Inverchoran, suggests shieling activity (the "airigh" element translates as "shieling" in Gaelic) and the remains of a group of 12 shieling huts are seen on a grassy flush beside the lochan. Platach Buidhe, above Achlorachan, means "yellow buttermilk" and Carn na Cloich Moire, southwest of Scatwell, is "hill of the bell of Mary", both hinting at the summer grazing of cattle. Carn na h-Annaite suggests a nearby religious site. Placenames can be descriptive of nature and the surrounding landscape, Drumandarroch, to the east of Scatwell in the lower glen, means "oak ridge" and suggests that there were far more of this type of tree than we see today, Creag na h-Iolaire means "crag of the eagles", Balnault "township of the burn" and Balnacraig, "township of the crag". There is no doubt that the study of the placenames in Strathconon provided an important contribution to our project but it is also a fascinating subject in itself.

---

[2] NAS E655/3/5 and MacPhail (1916) p332

*Fig 8.* The cup marked rock overlooking Scatwell, with plan above

*Fig 9.* Lower Strathconon with the dun at Glenmarksie in the foreground

# 3. The prehistoric period in Strathconon

It is quite probable that Strathconon was used as a routeway across the Highlands in the prehistoric period. A crossing via this route would avoid the treacherous sea journey around the north coast of Scotland. Several prehistoric sites had already been recorded in the glen before we embarked on our project and we were to add to these by finding a group of cup marked rocks and three hut circles, two with associated field systems.

Cup marked rocks date to the Neolithic period (4000BC-2500BC) and very little is known about them. They are often found above confluences of rivers or intersections of glens and usually have a good aspect to the south. One theory is that they marked the boundary of a territorial area, another that they marked a route. A fine group of cup marked rocks comprising one main boulder and at least ten "satellites" was found on the south facing slope to the north of Little Scatwell, above the confluence of the Rivers Meig and Conon. The main boulder has 54 cups and is situated on a terrace at GR NH 3956 5789. It has a good outlook to west and south but the area has been commercially forested and recently felled making underfoot conditions extremely treacherous. The discovery of these decorated rocks is evidence of people travelling in the glen, perhaps leading a nomadic life and not settling.

The south facing slopes around Carnoch were a particularly fruitful area for prehistoric remains. Even the name, meaning "place of cairns", is suggestive of early activity. Most of the prehistoric sites at this location probably date to the Bronze Age or Iron Age, and it has been suggested that the name Carnoch refers to the crannog[1] at the east end of Loch Beannacharain. This artificial island of stones is often submerged following the raising of the level of the loch. Crannogs were timber round houses built on wooden piles which were driven into small man made islands. A degree of protection was provided by the surrounding water and the structure would have given refuge in times of danger. Also from the same period of the Iron Age, and just below the present farmhouse at Carnoch, there is another type of fortified site - a dun[2]. Much of the original form of this site seems to have been disturbed by previous, probably antiquarian, exploration. The site has an overall diameter of about 24m and is situated on the summit of a small knoll on the north side of the river. Other duns or fortifications in the glen are at Carn nam Buaile[3] near Comrie, Glenmarksie[4] to the north of Scatwell and Creag Ruadh[5] on the hill to the north of the farmhouse at Glenmeinie. These fortifications indicate that the land was being contested during the Iron Age.

The new technology of bronzeworking was introduced around 2150 BC. Over a hundred years ago, in 1897, a stone axe mould[6] was discovered at Carnoch but its precise find spot was not recorded. Part of the tool kit of a craftsman working in bronze, the stone mould would have been used for casting flat axe heads for the local Early

[1] NMRS No NH25SW 003 at grid reference NH2437 5085
[2] NMRS No NH25SE 004 at grid reference NH 2507 5077
[3] NMRS No NH45NW 0005 at grid reference 4114 5669
[4] NMRS No NH35NE 0019 at grid reference NH 383 582
[5] NMRS No NH25SE 0003 at grid reference NH 2866 5343
[6] NMRS No NH25SW 0002

Bronze Age community at the time. Also in the same area a stone cist[7] was found in 1873. Again no details were recorded, other than that it was on a small mound. While the precise date of this find is unknown, these few clues are perhaps enough to suggest its interpretation as a Bronze Age grave, in which the body of the deceased would have been placed within the slab-built cist in a crouched position – another reminder of Strathconon's nameless prehistoric communities.

Complementing the sites at Carnoch already recorded we were to add a round house with a small field system during our project. Round houses are a feature of both the Bronze Age and the Iron Age. The site at Carnoch comprises one hut circle and at least two clearance cairns and is centred on GR NH 24695 51376, to the NW of the farmhouse. There may have been other features but subsequent activity on the slopes below will have destroyed them. The round house appears as a slightly raised circular heathery platform of about 8m internal diameter; the northern half is bounded by a well defined edge with some stone composition. There are two cairns close by, one of which is seen as an obvious green stony mound in heathery terrain. A further round house was located 2 miles to the west, near Scardroy, on a similar south facing slope. It is a recessed platform with substantial underbuild on its lower side and is situated on fertile ground which is covered by bracken in the summer.

*Fig 10.* The stone axe mould found at Carnoch in 1897 ©The Trustees of the National Museum of Scotland

Two rock shelters were recorded during the project and may have been used in prehistoric times but it is difficult to be certain of this. The rock shelters were found under large boulders, and their fine, well made, regular internal stonework is suggestive of an early period, but they may equally be of later date. At Soulmarksie a large flat slab just above the ruined farmstead has a small access passage at its rear leading to a small chamber. In the upper glen, opposite Inverchoran, and at the foot of a scree slope below Creag Iucharaidh a large pointed rock has a similar small chamber just 0.7m high underneath it.

[7] NMRS No NH25SE 0005 at grid reference NH 25 50 (an area of 1 square kilometre!)

*Fig 11*. The recessed platform above Scardroy which would have been occupied by a round house

*Fig 12*. Entrance to the rock shelter below Creag Iucharaidh

*Fig 13*. Internal stonework of the rock shelter at Soulmarksie

*Fig 14.* Francis Humberston Mackenzie, Lord Seaforth.
Image used by kind permission of the Trustees of The Highlanders' Museum

# 4. The rise of Clan Mackenzie and the fall of the Earl of Seaforth, their chief

The Mackenzie clan used to be thought of as a west coast clan which, during the late medieval period, had migrated eastward but it is now generally accepted that the kindred originally stemmed from Gilleoin of the Aird who had lands in the east in the earlier Medieval period. Documents for this time in Ross-shire have not survived and Grant (2000, p113-114) says

> It may well be that Gilleoin was like Somerled (of the Isles) in that he built up a great independent lordship in the early 12th century. The likelihood is that he expanded his power outwards from the Aird, around Beauly in the east, to fill what may have been a vacuum in southern Ross left by the retreat of Norse power during the previous century. And, just as with the kindred of Somerled after his death, his descendents fragmented into the three separate clans of Gillanders, Mackenzie and Matheson...... Thus the territory of Gilleon of the Aird's descendents can be seen as forming a contiguous block which straddled northern Scotland from the southern shores of the Beauly Firth across to the west coast. The parish of Kilmorack running up Strathfarrar and Strathglass adjoins Kintail and to the north the parishes of Urray (and Contin) similarly stretches westwards to Lochalsh....... since part of Strathconon seems to have been occupied by the Mackenzies in the early 14th century their lands may well have included this glen; there is a story of the wife of a 14th century Mackenzie chief who fell or was thrown over the bridge at Scatwell.

In the 12th and 13th centuries however, the Anglo-Norman Kings of Scotland, extending their influence into the north, gave the Lordship of the Aird to a loyal follower, John Bisset. This was a process which was happening in other parts of Scotland, Wales and Ireland. The descendents of Gilleoin of the Aird became a native kindred over whom feudal lordship was imposed. But the territory of the Lordship of the Aird was "border country", Norman control did not extend to the west coast and it would appear that the native kindred of Gilleoin retreated to their lands in the west.

The Mackenzies retained their interest in the lands to the east through the next centuries for, in 1463, they were granted lands known as the Braes of Ross which included Killin, Garve and Kinlochluichart by John Macdonald, Earl of Ross and Lord of the Isles and in 1477 they were given a charter from the Crown, not only confirming them in the lands of Kintail, but granting them the lands of Strathconon, Strathgarve and Strathbraan. The clan had established strongholds on the crannogs, or fortified islands, of Loch Achilty and Loch Kinellen, near Strathpeffer. The Mackenzie chiefs and their cadet branches became firmly established in Ross-shire over the next century. Their lands on the west and east coasts were linked geographically by direct routes which passed through Strathconon and Strathbran.

The history of Strathconon in the late medieval period is covered by Aonghas MacCoinnich in "Strathconon and the Mackenzies in the sixteenth and seventeenth centuries", Chapter 5 of this publication. By 1700 the estates of the clan chief, Mackenzie of Kintail, now the Earl of Seaforth, included not only Strathconon, Kintail, Lochalsh and Lochcarron but also the Island of Lewis. In order to understand the later situation of the 19th Century and the eventual outcomes in Strathconon, it is necessary to explore something of the history of the Mackenzie chiefs and their policy of military recruitment in this later period.

In the early 18th century the royalist William Mackenzie, 5th Earl of Seaforth and Chief of the Clan Mackenzie, took up the cause of James Stewart, the "Old Pretender". He played a major part in the uprising of 1715 and, after its suppression at the battle of Sherrifmuir, he fled to France where he died in exile in 1740. His eldest son supported the Protestant succession and the Government in the 1745 rebellion and as a result his grandson, Kenneth Mackenzie, created 6th Earl of Seaforth, was allowed to purchase back the forfeited estates in 1771. But the restoration of the Seaforth lands came at a bleak time in Highland history. The government in its determination to avoid another Jacobite rising had set about dismantling the clan system with uncompromising severity. The disarming of the Highlanders and their deliberate suppression brought a time of misery. Faced with economic ruin and the destruction of the traditional way of life, many clan chiefs realized that one way to provide employment and bring money to their tenants was by raising regiments of Highland infantry.

Military conflict had figured large in Highland clan histories; inter-clan rivalries and feuds had been endemic since early times. Most feuds were triggered by disputes over land possession and the feud was one of the ways by which aggressive clans could expand, taking land from their weaker rivals. The provision of land by a clan chief in return for military service from his clansmen is a well known aspect of Scottish history. Traditionally the land belonged to the clan, the chief was the patriarch of the clan, he provided for his clansmen by supplying them with land and in return the clansmen would give their loyalty and military service. Many chiefs encouraged a large population specifically to provide a large fighting force. But by the late 18th century the situation had changed, the uprising of 1745 and Culloden had come and gone and there was a more peaceful period. The whole country was involved in military conflicts overseas and recruits were needed for the British Army to fight in the American and French Revolutionary Wars and for unrest in the colonies. From 1778 Kenneth Mackenzie and his successors were to raise several regiments from their clansmen for service in these conflicts. Kenneth commanded his 78th Highlanders, also known as the "Ross-shire Buffs", until his death on a voyage to India in 1781. Thomas Mackenzie Humberston, his cousin, succeeded him as chief of the clan, but died of wounds in Bombay in 1783. He was followed by his brother Francis Humberston Mackenzie who in 1793 raised a further regiment from Clan Mackenzie lands. It is probable that the indecisiveness and confused policies of this Earl of Seaforth, executed, some would say, with the best of intentions, were one of the factors which led to the unhappy state of affairs which was later to develop in Strathconon in the 19th century. Dr John Mackenzie (1803-1886), whose father Mackenzie of Gairloch (and Conan) was a great friend of Francis Humberston Mackenzie, described him

Lord Seaforth, a friend in his youth of the future King George IV, a man of many talents (in spite of being deaf and having a severe speech defect) was distinguished in public life, but was wildly extravagant and notorious for the financial mismanagement of his vast estates (Byam Shaw, 1988, p66).

Finlay McKichan argues very convincingly that Seaforth was slower than other proprietors in abandoning traditional attitudes (McKichen, 2007). McKichen concludes that Seaforth was interested in the heritage of his clan, that he took patriarchal pride in raising regiments and was unwilling to displace small tenants to make way for large sheep farms. Seaforth was concerned to restore and maintain the political influence of his family's interests in Ross-shire and he opposed pressure from his advisers to sell traditional clan lands in Kintail. Attempting to combine traditional and commercial objectives at that time was fraught with difficulty. It is easy to comment in hindsight, but at the time Seaforth was unwilling to accept that the roles of chief and capitalist landlord were incompatible and he fought a losing battle to reconcile the two.

Over 1,000 men were raised by Seaforth for his 2nd battalion in 1793. They came principally from Clan Mackenzie, about half from the cadet branches of Gairloch, Scatwell, Kilcoy, Applecross and Redcastle and half from Seaforth's own estates of Kintail, Lochalsh and Lewis. No direct evidence of recruits from Strathconon has been found but it seems impossible to think that they were not involved. Clan Macrae of Kintail had long been faithful followers of the Seaforth family and was known as Mackenzie's "shirt of mail" or bodyguard; on occasions the name of Macrae was so prevalent in the regiment that it was frequently referred to as the regiment of the "Macraes".

> Recruitment and the military employment it guaranteed can be seen as an economic strategy born out of the landlord's search for additional relatively secure income….. In 1795 the Seaforth family debt stood ar £90,994 and by 1800 had reached £108,000. By contrast the income from the Lewis, Kintail, Lochalsh, Glensheal (and Strathconon) estates, which constituted the bulk of the Seaforth property, totalled only £9,950. Cheap borrowing had traditionally provided the answer to the Scottish landlord's debt problems and lack of capital, but the American and French wars had drained available credit into lucrative government stocks and shares. (McKillop, 2000, p136)

Seaforth was to achieve his ambition of raising his family's profile within the north by his military policies. His estates gained the reputation for retaining large reserves of population and his recruiting efforts resulted in his being elected MP for Ross-shire from 1784 to 1790 and Lord Lieutenant of Ross-shire in 1797. In addition he received the governorship of the Barbados in 1800.

Recruiting for the military however came at a price. Seaforth had promised to supply his clansmen with leases of land at reduced rents when they returned from military service. The late 18th century was a time of commercialism and there was pressure to develop sheep farming which involved incoming sheep farmers with experience. Landowners were faced with a dilemma, how could they accommodate their old tenantry returning from the wars and at the same time introduce sheep farming? The situation on Seaforth's estates was difficult

(Military) recruitments ability to retard the spread of sheep farming was apparent on the Earl of Seaforth's estates of Glensheal, Kintail and Lochalsh in the mid 1790s. The extent of the concessions obtained by the tenantry became a major complicating factor when attempts were made from 1794 onwards to sell Glensheal. Seven year leases and what was recognized as a low rental made a sale difficult to complete and it was only sold in 1801 when the leases given at the time of recruiting expired and even then at 10% less than the asking price of £42,000. Furthermore the largely positive response of the tenantry in Kintail and Glensheal to recruiting for the 78th Highland Regiment had elicited a promise from Seaforth that when the leases granted in 1794 expired in 1801 local tenant families would be preferred over strangers if they offered appropriate rents. Thus in 1800 when a Lieutenant Macdonald of Lochaber asked for a sheep farm in Glensheal, Mackenzie of Fairburn, advised Seaforth "In the first place I would call on the present tenants for their proposals". The situation was summarized by an adviser to Seaforth - "It would certainly be more advantageous for the farms to have been let each to a single tenant, but this would have left twenty-one totally unprovided for. We found ourselves tied up by an express promise given at the former set to give the tenants a preference to strangers (McKillop 2000, p160).

Seaforth's answer was to let some of the tacks to his old tenantry as multiple tenancies for sheep farming, a practice that was against the trend. In the late 18th century the introduction of sheep farming with the process of competitive bidding for leases and the creation of large single tenant farms meant that club farms of multiple tenants were largely being eliminated. In Seaforth's estate of Lewis John Headrick, an itinerant agricultural commentator reported that in the year 1800 multiple tenancies were the norm. In 1801 Glenshiel was divided into six farms; new leases required sheep farming and were given to the most promising of the existing farmers as multiple tenancies of between two and four farmers. Most of the original tenants were accommodated and the rental brought in was doubled, but even so there were casualties; eleven tenants, "those that seemed unfit for following the sheep system", were concentrated at Morvich. In Kintail the surplus population was moved to the village of Dornie.

The situation was paralleled in Strathconon in 1803; at this time the glen was in the hands of a group of Trustees with Mackenzie of Fairburn at the helm. It had been divided into seven sheepwalks, five being rented by multiple or club tenants from the old tenantry and two by incoming sheep farmers. James Hogg (1888) writes of his travels in 1803

He (a fellow traveller) informed me that all the extensive estate (of Strathconon) was let to sheep farmers saving a small division at the lower end, which the General had reserved for the accommodation of such of the natives as could not dispose of themselves to better advantage (A similar situation to that of Morvich in Kintail and Dornie)

The population level in Strathconon was large even before the general upsurge of the late 18th and early 19th centuries and by his policies Seaforth maintained this large population. The fate of multiple tenancies and the population of Strathconon is explored in Chapter 9.

Reflecting on his actions later, Seaforth commented that he acted against advice because "I was so anxious to keep together the people I looked on as heritably attached to my family". On his death in 1815 Francis Humberston Mackenzie left debts estimated to be £148,399. By this time significant parts of the estate in the west had been sold, but his land sales had been insufficient to restore his financial position. The direct male line of his family had come to an end and his heir and daughter Mary was obliged to sell off more and more of the Seaforth lands. By her death in 1862 most of the estate had gone except in the vicinity of Brahan. It was a difficult time; there is no doubt that the small tenants of the Seaforth estates suffered from the commercialism of the Highlands, but their clan chief also suffered and went down with them too.

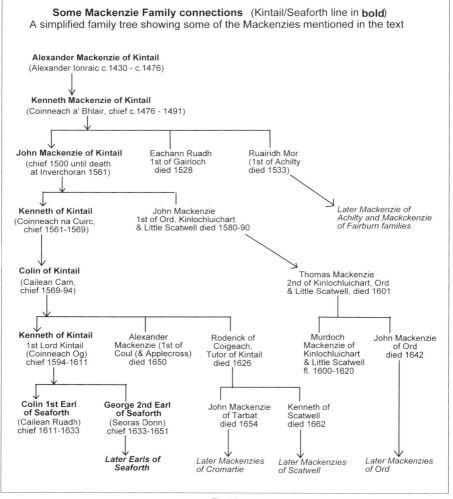

**Some Mackenzie Family connections** (Kintail/Seaforth line in **bold**)
A simplified family tree showing some of the Mackenzies mentioned in the text

**Alexander Mackenzie of Kintail**
(Alexander Ionraic c.1430 - c.1476)

**Kenneth Mackenzie of Kintail**
(Coinneach a' Bhlair, chief c.1476 - 1491)

**John Mackenzie of Kintail**
(chief 1500 until death
at Inverchoran 1561)

Eachann Ruadh
1st of Gairloch
died 1528

Ruairidh Mor
(1st of Achilty
died 1533)

**Kenneth of Kintail**
(Coinneach na Cuirc,
chief 1561-1569)

John Mackenzie
1st of Ord, Kinlochluichart
& Little Scatwell died 1580-90

*Later Mackenzie of
Achilty and Mackckenzie
of Fairburn families*

**Colin of Kintail**
(Cailean Cam,
chief 1569-94)

Thomas Mackenzie
2nd of Kinlochluichart, Ord
& Little Scatwell, died 1601

**Kenneth of Kintail**
1st Lord Kintail
(Coinneach Og)
chief 1594-1611

Alexander
Mackenzie (1st of
Coul (& Applecross)
died 1650

Roderick of
Coigeach,
Tutor of Kintail
died 1626

Murdoch
Mackenzie of
Kinlochluichart
& Little Scatwell
fl. 1600-1620

John Mackenzie
of Ord
died 1642

**Colin 1st Earl
of Seaforth**
(Cailean Ruadh)
chief 1611-1633

**George 2nd Earl
of Seaforth**
(Seoras Donn)
chief 1633-1651

John Mackenzie
of Tarbat
died 1654

Kenneth of
Scatwell
died 1662

**Later Earls of
Seaforth**

*Later Mackenzies
of Cromartie*

*Later Mackenzies
of Scatwell*

*Later Mackenzies
of Ord*

*Fig 15.*

# 5. Strathconon and the Mackenzies in the sixteenth and seventeenth centuries

## by Aonghas MacCoinnich, University of Strathclyde

This is an abridged version of an essay, "Strathconon, Scatwell and the Mackenzies in the written record, c1463–c1700". The full version, expanded and fully referenced, is published in the report of Phase 3 of the NOSAS Strathconon Project and can be seen on the NOSAS website at

http://www.nosas.co.uk/documents/Site%20Records/SC%203.pdf

and also on the Highland HER website at

http://her.highland.gov.uk/SingleResult.aspx?uid='EHG3309'

Although some writers have considered the earlier history of Ross, these studies tend to focus on dynastic and political events and not much is know about the internal workings of Ross-shire far less Strathconon in the historical record prior to the end of the fifteenth century. Strathconon, strategically situated in central Ross, was the key to the control of the earldom of Ross in that possession of these lands secured control of the few good access routes from coast to coast. The earldom of Ross and the possession thereof was pivotal to the fortunes of the Macdonald Lords of the Isles who were fatally undermined by their loss of the area to the Stewart monarchy in 1475. This essay will consider the Strathconon and Scatwell area from the time of its earliest appearance in the historical record at the end of the fifteenth century and go on to concentrate on the area in the sixteenth and early seventeenth centuries. An attempt will be made to pull together a variety of written sources in order to try to build up a picture of the area in this period inasmuch as the evidence will allow. These lands, Strathconon and Scatwell, which form the focus of this investigation, were a small part of a much wider estate that was controlled in this period, c.1463 to 1700 by the Mackenzies of Kintail / Seaforth.

## I  Early mentions of the Strathconon area, and the Mackenzies ante 1508

The earliest mention of 'Strathconon' is a reference to a (now lost) grant by King Robert I to Earl Hugh of Ross around 1309, but the earliest substantial body of historical evidence dates from the later fifteenth century. The earliest surviving credible reference to a Mackenzie in the historical record is to Alexander (Alasdair 'Ionraic') Mackenzie in 1463/4. This document, a charter to Alexander from John Macdonald of Islay, Lord of the Isles and Earl of Ross, does not survive. Moreover, this charter (1463/4) would appear to have been the earliest title deed that was in the possession of Colin Mackenzie, the first earl of Seaforth around 1627, the chief of that name, when a notary made an inventory of Seaforth's charters. This inventory survives and is preserved in the Cromartie Papers in the National Archives of Scotland. This inventory is headed with the earliest and first title deed held by the Mackenzies: a note of a charter by John Macdonald Lord of Islay and Earl of Ross to his 'cusing' or cousin, Alexander Mackenzie of Kintail as follows

> In the ffirst Ane chairtor gevin be Johne of Ila Earle of Ros and [Lord] of the Yllis
> to his cusing Alex[ande]r Mckenze of Kintaill off the fyve merk lands of Ki[llin ?]
> the fyve merk lands of Garve. The tua m[er]k land of Corriewulzie, the thrie

29

m[er]k land of Kenlochluichart, the tua merk land of Garbat, the tua m[er]k land of Dalnatwa, the four merk land of Auchlask, the four m[er]k land of Taag lyand within the Earldom of Ros and She[rri]ffdome of Innernes haldin of the earles of Ros be s[e]rvice of ward & relief and is daitit at Dingwall the sevint day of Ja[nua]r 1463.

Alexander Mackenzie was succeeded sometime around 1479 by his son Kenneth. Alexander had held his lands from the Macdonald earls of Ross. However, King James III (1460-1488), forfeited the earldom of Ross in 1475, taking it from the Macdonalds and the Stewart monarchs struggled for over a quarter of a century to realise their claims to the earldom against Macdonald counter-claims. Such was the context for Kenneth's short, bloody period as clan chief (c.1479-1491). Kenneth was known in Gaelic as 'Coinneach a' Bhlàir' (of the battle) and seems to have turned on his erstwhile allies, the Macdonalds, against whom he fought at least two battles in Ross-shire, Lag a' Bhrèid sometime in the 1480s which he lost, and Blàr na Pàirce (c.1489-91) which he won. This final battle broke the Macdonald stranglehold on Easter Ross, resulting eventually in Crown domination of the area and a great increase in the power of the Mackenzies.

The Mackenzies were, as we have seen above, strongly associated with the Strathconon area in the Macdonald charter of 1463. This association is confirmed in surviving documentation associated with Kenneth (Coinneach a' Bhlàir †c. 1433-91), who between 1479 and 1487 claimed that he had a 'right' to the lands of 'Eskadellis,' (Eskdale) 'Meyn' (Glenmeanie) in 'Straquhonane' and 'Innerquhonray' (Inverchoran), Kenloch Benquharane (Ceann Loch Beanncharain, near Scardroy) all in Strathconon. The claim to these lands, based perhaps on continued possession, may have stretched back over several generations.

## II The strategic importance of the Strathconon and Scatwell area

Barbara Crawford has plausibly suggested that the Strathconon corridor may have been an important strategic east-west thoroughfare in Viking times (as no doubt was Strathgarve-Strathbran). The importance of these straths in central Ross in controlling east-west access was not lost either on the Macdonald earls of Ross (c.1411-1475) or on the kings of Scots (1475-). Strathconon seems to have been one of the routes used to access the east coast by the Macdonald forces that tried to reclaim the earldom of Ross sometime around 1490. An account in a Mackenzie history indicates that Macdonald forces used the same route shortly afterwards to retreat home to the west following their heavy defeat at the hands of a Mackenzie led force at Blàr na Pàirce (c.1489-90) near modern Strathpeffer. One party of retreating Macdonalds, were, it seems caught by pursuing Mackenzies at Inverchoran; some were killed there and others escaped. The strategic importance of Strathconon and adjacent lands which had been recognised by the Macdonald grant of 1463 of lands in central Ross to Alexander Mackenzie was paralleled by the grant issued by James IV of exactly the same lands to Alexander's grandson, John Mackenzie of Kintail in 1508/9. The placing of the Mackenzies athwart such strategic passes, by granting them the lands of Strathconon, Strath Bran, Strath Gairbh and Strath Mòr enabled them to control movement through the straths.

## III Ownership of the Strathconon area post 1508/9

James III had, arguably, instigated much of the chaos that visited the west Highlands and Islands due to his attempt to oust the Macdonalds from Ross in 1475. It took thirty-three years before his successor James IV achieved a measure of control in the area, although Macdonald discontent died hard and lingered for generations. In the earldom of Ross the function of holding future Macdonald rebellions at bay was largely performed for the Crown by the Mackenzies, who from now on had a close and mutually beneficial relationship with the Stewart monarchs. They were confirmed in their possession of much the same lands as they had held as tenants of the Macdonalds, only now, from 1508, they were tenants in chief, holding their lands directly of the crown rather than as subordinates of another clan.

The Mackenzie hold of the lands of Strathconon, Kintail, and adjacent lands became stronger during the sixteenth century as the clan, favoured by the Crown, and benefitting from competent leadership not least that of John of Kintail, (chief c.1500-1561), strengthened their grip of these and other lands in Ross-shire, often at the expense of less fortunate neighbours. Indeed it was at Inverchoran in Strathconon that John Mackenzie of Kintail, ended his career, dying aged around 80 in January 1561. A succession of deeds name the lands of Strathconon as an integral, if a small, part of the burgeoning Mackenzie 'empire' bound up (from 1508-9) with the lands of Kintail as part of the barony of Eilean Donnan.

While many nowadays might consider the moors and hills of these lands a 'wasteland' or wilderness, they were a keenly contested resource in the sixteenth and seventeenth century in terms of not only their hunting and fishing potential but especially their value as summer grazing. Such resources were jealously guarded and neighbours on both sides of the boundaries were keenly aware of the extent of their rights. The Tutor of Lovat at Beauly in June 1589, gave the lands of 'Ardnicrask' to a Donald Maciver and his brother John to keep the [Fraser] marches along the river Orrin between Ardnacrask and up into the wilds of Coire Chairbre secure 'against the Stratchounin men.' Of these 'Strathconon men' perhaps the one who attracts the most in the way of historical 'column inches', although for matters relating to areas outwith Strathconon, was 'Torcal Conanach' or Torquil MacLeod (c.1535-c.1612), son of Ruairidh Macleod of Lewis by one of his spouses, Janet Mackenzie. This unfortunate Torquil MacLeod was the unsuccesful Mackenzie-backed claimant for the lordship of Lewis. He was known as 'Torcal Conanach,' due to his being raised and fostered in the region of Strathconon. Torquil's oide or foster father was his maternal uncle, John Mackenzie of Kinlochluichart (or Ord), second son of John Mackenzie of Kintail (chief 1500-61)

## IV Cailean Càm's Estate Accounts, 1569

While it is clear that boundaries of estates were keenly observed and contested, the activity within these bounds is not always clear. An estate account prepared for Colin Mackenzie of Kintail (or Cailean Càm), the chief of the Mackenzies of Kintail (1569-94) survives for 1569. This supplies us with some fascinating vignettes of life on the large estates of the Mackenzies of Kintail including Strathconon. The lands of

'Strathconon' returned rents to the chief in that year together with separate returns for 'Scatoll M[e]ikle' and 'Litill Skatoll.' A man referred to as 'mc Dow Moir' in Scatwell made a payment of 6s 8d in lieu of the heriot horse he owed his chief following, presumably, his father's death. The 'heriot' was a sort of 'death duty' levied in Scotland at that time whereby the clan-chief could take the best horse or cow of the deceased from the deceased's next of kin, as a return to the chief for a lifetime's protection of his clansman. Despite the evident circulation of cash, payments in kind remained common. The taxes of Kintail and Strathconon were paid to the estate in merts ('marts' or cattle). Strathconon supplied four that year which were then sent onwards to the port of Cromarty. Other cattle were sent sporadically to the chief on demand.

Ferchir mcConchie Dow was the 'officiar' of Strathconon and he disbursed 40s in 1569 which was given to the 'blawaris of the Irne.' The 'irne' or iron referred to here is unclear. 'Blawaris' of the iron would seem to imply that some tenants on this part of the estate had a duty, perhaps, to man bellows in the production of iron. Forty shillings seems like quite a large sum. It is unclear where this iron was being worked; the Loch Maree area to the west would seem more likely than the immediate environs of Strathconon and this area was parcelled together with the Loch Maree area in terms of estate management at this time (see discussion of iron works below).

Further down the glen, John mcConchie Moir, 'officiar' of Skatwell in 1569, paid 13s 4d for a horse hide to be used on the curra[ch] or coracle presumably used for crossing the river Conon. Although pitch is not named in conjunction with this entry it does appear elsewhere in the account and one hopes that John's currach was watertight. In any event it appears that the ferry at Scatwell for which the curach, presumably, was used was a profitable concern as it generated enough revenue to be liable to taxes to the tune of 20s in 1588. It was not an occupation that was without its hazards as crossing the river by boat could be a risky business. Mr James Fraser reported nearly 100 years later, in 1667, that twenty-two persons had drowned in the Conon due to overloading of the ferry, which sounds like a larger craft than the earlier coracle.

### V Cailean Càm's last will and testament, 1594 and Jane Ross's testament, 1604
The rental of 1569 is a document related to the beginning of Cailean's time as chief and the next document that sheds light on matters in the Scatwell and Strathconon corners of his estates appears at the death of Cailean Càm at Redcastle in 1594. Cailean's last will and testament includes a lengthy list of debts owing to the deceased and this included items related to Strathconon. The sum of £148 was owed to Colin's estate in both money and victual (beir) by 'Tormot mcIwer (Tormod MacÌomhair), Donald McEwir (Dòmhnall MacÌomhair), and the remanent tenantis & occupiaris of the ground and lands of Strath[ch]onane.' The lands of Strathconon were parcelled together with the lands of Kinlochewe in terms of another commodity appearing in the inventory: iron. A John mcCondochie (Iain mac Dhonnchaidh), Donald mcGillespie (Dòmhnall mac Gilleasbuig) and a Thomas mc[Inglas] (Tòmas mac Iain Glais), tenants and occupiers of the lands and ground of Strathconon and Kinlochewe 'paid the dutie on 1500 cleiffis of irne' to Cailean Càm their chief, coming to a sum of £1500.

This £1500 was a substantial sum, amounting to 10% of the estate's income, and Cailean's estate compares favourably with that of his fellow nobles. He was a very wealthy man by the standards of the day and this income from iron was a significant sum. Colin was succeeded by his son Kenneth Mackenzie of Kintail. Kenneth married Jane Ross, a daughter of Ross of Balnagowan in 1593. Jane died in 1604 and her last will and testament included reference to the payment of mails or rents due to her from the part of the Mackenzie estates bestowed on her. This included a reference to a John mcConneil (Iain mac Dhòmhnaill), Donald mac Ewir (Dòmhnall mac Ìomhair) and other tenants in Strathconon in regard of the meal and bere they owed the estate. A separate entry appeared for those who were to work on the iron in both the Strathconon and Kinlochewe areas. Jane Ross's testament in 1604 showed some of the same names which had appeared in her late father in law's testament ten years earlier: John mcConndochie (Iain mac Dhonnchaidh), Donald mcGilleis (Dòmhnall mac Gill'Iosa), and Thomas mcInglas (Tòmas mac Iain Glais), all named as tenants in Strathconon.

The recurrence of Strathconon tenants in an entry related to iron in 1569, 1594 and 1604 (as discussed above) raises some interesting questions. Although it has long been recognised that there was significant iron working on the ground in the Loch Maree area, the linkage of this area with Strathconon in connection with iron working is new. In terms of the place-names, almost all in the Strathconon area are of Gaelic origin and some of the Strathconon area, such as 'ruadh', 'mèinne' and 'iarann' are suggestive of iron working but this might be reading too much into limited evidence. The dearth of source materials makes such interpretation of the place-name evidence very tempting. Scardroy, or An Sgàrd Ruaidh, for instance, means a reddish scree - a reddish marking on rocks, indicating the presence (perhaps?) of traces of iron ore although this seems difficult to prove without geological analysis. The name element 'Mèinne,' (Glenmeanie) however, would seem on the face of it to signify a 'mine.' Although the British Geological Survey's report on the area would not appear to support economically viable concentrations of ore nowadays, this might not always have been the case. What is economically marginal nowadays might have been feasible with a large labour pool in the very different economic climate of the sixteenth century. This being so, and with documentary sources telling us that Strathconon men were engaged in iron working, but being unable to satisfactorily identify iron-working sites in Strathconon, it does raise a further question. Were people from the Strathconon lands used as a labour force in iron production activity in the Loch Maree area, for which we have better evidence, or were they engaged in iron-working closer to home ?

## VI The economy
The economy of the area based on the strength of these two documents, despite the significant reference to iron, and a significant salmon fishery, was based largely on cattle production. Perhaps not surprisingly bere (barley) and meal are listed as an exaction from the tenants of Strathconon in 1604, which implies the existence of mills necessary for the production of such meal together with activities attested elsewhere on the Mackenzies' estates such as brewing and presumably distilling. While there was

cultivation in some sections of the strath, most of this land was marginal agricultural land. Cattle production, rather than arable farming, was the main focus of activity on the Strathconon section of the wider Kintail/Seaforth estates. This is reflected in the explicit mention in a number of conveyancing documents (and evident in the place-names) of grazings and sheilings. These place-names would not be mentioned in such documents unless there was a distinct economic angle to the transaction and we have - unless future research clarifies this - little to quantify the precise nature of the cattle-rearing operation on the Kintail/Seaforth estates, including Strathconon, other than confidently saying it was substantial. Research by Dr Alasdair Ross on the Stratha'an estate, and on Breadalbane lands where documentation does exist clearly indicates the importance of such intensive cattle-farming on highland estates during this period. It would seem that the Mackenzie management of their estates, including the Strathconon area, with an emphasis on cattle farming on marginal lands, closely paralleled what was happening elsewhere in Highland Scotland during this period.

## VII The lands and the church

Colin Mackenzie the first earl of Seaforth (c.1594-1633) was praised by late seventeenth-century clan chroniclers for his piety. He laid the foundation, apparently, for a church in Strathconon of which the walls are 'still to be seen in Main in Strathconon, the walls being built above the height of a man above the foundation, and he had a mind to endow it further had he lived longer.' By the time of the Old and New Statistical Accounts, of 1793 and 1834, there was no mention of such a church, any previous building having been superseded by the new churches at Kinlochluichart and at Strathconon built in 1821 and 1830.

The lands of Strathconon fell under the parochial watch of the vicars or ministers of Contin and, seemingly, Urray and Fodderty. Of these parishes not too much is known prior to the Reformation. There is a record of a man surnamed 'Fores' ('For[b]es' or 'Forres'?) as the incumbent of Contin parish prior to 1550, when he was succeeded by a David Stewart. A Mr Robert Burnet was the parson of Contin – or at least in receipt of the parochial income at the time of the Reformation, 1560. It seems that formal clerical provision may have been patchy in the Strathconon area if not in Scatwell. This impression of a patchy clerical provision for Strathconon around the Reformation and earlier is reinforced when the historical record does become fuller during the seventeenth century. Dingwall Presbytery records from the latter part of the seventeenth century give us more information about Strathconon and its difficulties in securing the services of a minister due to the area's reliance on surrounding parishes. Mr Farquhar MacLennan, minister of Fodderty and Mr Donald MacRae, minister at Urray were ordered in 1649 to go and preach in Strathconon as this 'was incumbent on them.' The moderator of the Dingwall Presbytery in a meeting of 1666, commented that all the ministers present were 'diligent in their preaching and catechising save that Strathconon alone was neglected.' The brethren ordered Mr George Cumine, minister of Urray (1658-1705) and Mr Donald Ross, minister of Contin (1651-1674) to take action regarding the serving of Strathconon. Mr Donald Ross seems to have acted on this and was recorded as having preached at Strathconon in 1664. The presbytery did record that they were mindful that it was difficult for ministers to serve at Strathconon, and they seem to have built a house for itinerant ministers visiting the area.

## VIII The language, naming patterns and river systems

The language of Strathconon for most of the late medieval and early modern period was Gaelic. As recently as 1891 three quarters of the remaining 249 residents of Strathconon still spoke Gaelic. Only 6.9 % (or five persons) in the Strathconon area still spoke Gaelic according to the census of 2001. We are largely reliant on place name evidence for Gaelic usage in the area prior to 1700.

Another indication of language usage can be seen in the personal names of the tenantry recorded in the Forfeited Estates rental of 1719-24 and in the personal names noted, above, in the account from 1569 and the testaments of 1594 and 1604. They did not all necessarily have 'surnames' as we would know them. This custom of formal surnames was a feature of the Scots and English-speaking world. Nevertheless, had it been put to tenants on the Seaforth estates in an external setting what their names were, they might well have replied, 'Mackenzie,' 'MacRae,' 'MacLeay' or 'MacLennan,' but these were 'external' names that were not widely used within the Seaforth estates, and they were little used by the tenants themselves prior to the nineteenth century. The names that mattered to them were family names, patronymics and by-names.

Most of the rest of the direct evidence available to W. J. Watson (Watson was himself a native Gaelic speaker from the Evanton area) around 1900, when Gaelic speech was still common, has gone. Watson, however, together with the place name materials, recorded an enigmatic local saying.

Abhainn Mìg tre Srath-chonuinn
Abhainn Conuinn tre Srath-bhràinn
Abhainn Dubh-chuileagach tre Srath-ghairbh
Tri aibhnichean gun tairbh iad sin.

[translated as: *The River Meig through Strathconon, The River Conon through Strathbran, The river of Black nooks through Strathgarve; three rivers without profit, these*]

While the reason for this verse is not clear to me, the sentiment in it, perhaps ironic, that the rivers were without profit, is contradicted by all the other evidence which suggests that the river systems were harvested to good effect on the Mackenzie/Seaforth estate. The recurrent appearance of fishings, lochs and rivers in title deeds indicates that this was a valuable resource that was being actively exploited, implying the use of river systems for mill-lades, yairs (fishtraps) and weirs. While the destination of the end product from the rivers, presumably salted and barrelled salmon is unknown, the fact that they were using 'Hamburg' measures in this period (the sixteenth century) suggests they may have been sent to a Baltic market.

## IX The Mackenzie families of Coul, Kinlochluichart & Ord

As noted above, the lands of Strathconon were an integral part of the estate of the Mackenzies of Kintail/Seaforth. As the sixteenth and seventeenth centuries progressed, and the Mackenzie clan amassed land and power, cadet families such as the Mackenzies of Ord, Kinlochluichart, Coul, Scatwell slowly established themselves as landed families while remaining (in this period anyway) under the wing of the senior family or 'chief' of Kintail/Seaforth who was their feudal superior. At some point in the sixteenth century John Mackenzie of Ord, brother of Kenneth Mackenzie of Kintail, became possessor of the lands of Kinlochluichart and probably Strathconon. John of Ord was a shadowy figure about whom little is now known, his son, however, Thomas Mackenzie of Kinlochluichart appears more frequently in surviving documentation from about 1580. Thomas had seemingly lost 400 'scheip, mearis and horsis' (sheep mares and horses) which were lifted from him in Kinlochluichart by followers or 'servandis' of George Ross of Balnagownan in March 1590/1. Thomas Mackenzie of Kinlochluichart died sometime between 1598 and 1600. He was twice married. His eldest son from his first marriage, Murdo (fl. 1600-20), succeeded him in the lands of Kinlochluichart while his eldest son from his second marriage, John of Ord (fl. 1600-42), followed his father in the lands of Ord.

## X The Mackenzies of Ord and the new Mackenzies of Scatwell

John of Ord (1607-42) and his spouse Isobel Cuthbert did not get all of his father's lands. His elder half-brother Murdo (fl.1611-19), seems to have succeeded to the lands of Scatwell formerly held by his father and, confusingly, also seems to have retained the designations of 'Kinlochluichart' and 'Ord.' Murdo had a close connection with Roderick Mackenzie of Coigeach, known as the tutor of Kintail (progenitor of the earls of Cromartie). Although Murdo was married to a Catherine Mackenzie, the couple seem to have been childless. Murdo and Catherine fostered Kenneth, Roderick of Coigeach's son and, in a deed of 1619, resigned these lands of Scatwell to the young Kenneth in exchange for 'certane sums of money and good deeds' performed for him by Roderick, on the proviso that Murdo and his wife would themselves remain childless. This document is of interest as it clearly states that Colin Mackenzie, Lord Kintail, was the feudal superior of these lands. This arrangement was tied in with the 'half davoch' lands of Little Scatwell including the river and loch fishings. These lands remained in the hands of Kenneth's descendants, the Scatwell family, for many generations after this (1619-).

## XI The Mackenzies of Scatwell, Ord & Kinlochluichart

Kenneth (†1662), the first of this branch of Little Scatwell was succeeded by three of his sons in turn, the first two dying young. In 1688 Kenneth Mackenzie of Scatwell having outlived his brothers, succeeded his father as heir male in the lands of Little Scatwell, with its pool and salmon fishing and the lands of Kinlochluichart with fishing, illustrating that the seventeenth century lairds clearly saw the rivers as a resource worth exploiting. Kenneth married Lillias Mackenzie, heiress to the lands of her father, Roderick Mackenzie of Findon, who inherited her father's lands in 1693. This inheritance gradually drew the family's centre of gravity away from Scatwell. According to Alexander Mackenzie (1894) the family removed from Lochluichart to Findon (in the Black Isle) in 1696, although retaining an interest in the original lands until 1844.

The proliferation of Mackenzie cadet branches makes tracing these families tricky, however. This is compounded by the presence of another, lesser known, cadet family – the Mackenzie family of Meikle Scatwell. Mr John Mackenzie (†1620) minister of Dingwall held the lands of Tolly, which he passed on to his son Murdo. Murdo succeeded Mr John in these lands with the addition of Meikle Scatwell, granted him by Kenneth Mackenzie of Kintail in 1608. This family continued to hold these lands of Meikle Scatwell, until the family faded out of the historical record about 1700. While the focus in these last sections has been on cadet families it is worth noting that the senior family, the Mackenzies of Kintail/Seaforth, retained an interest in the Strathconon area from our earliest records in the mid fifteenth century until their estate was also broken up in the mid nineteenth century.

## Conclusion

By the end of the period under consideration here, at the end of the seventeenth century, as at the beginning, the lands of Strathconon and Scatwell were under the control of the Mackenzies. While the Kintail branch of the family remained dominant, the families of Tarbat/Cromartie, Scatwell and Coul became increasingly important. Iron seemingly played an important if little understood role in the local economy, while salmon-fishing, agriculture and especially cattle rearing were all mainstays of the economy on the Mackenzies estates during the seventeenth century. Considerable research remains to be done on the untapped wealth of source material from the seventeenth century in collections of family papers and in official collections such as the Registers of Deeds and the Sasines in the National Archives of Scotland that would do much to illuminate patterns of landholding and conditions in the Strathconon and Scatwell area in the seventeenth century. Such a detailed survey is outwith the scope of this more limited investigation, which, nevertheless, does offer a framework for further historical and archaeological research on the Strathconon area.

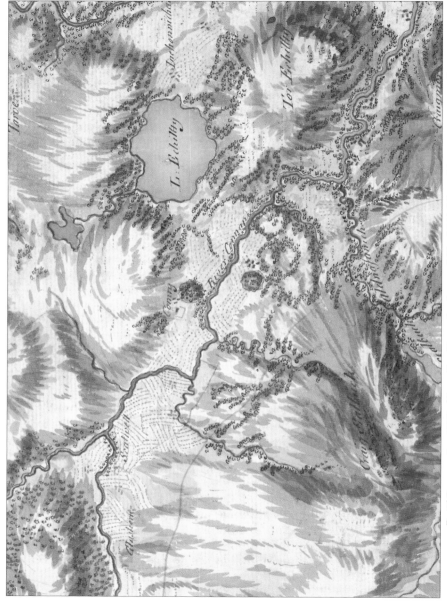

*Fig 16.* Roy map circa. 1750 of Scatwell and Lower Strathconon © The British Library. Licensor www.scran.ac.uk

# 6. The history of Scatwell and the lower glen

The name Scatwell without doubt has Norse origins, but its meaning is illusive. Some believe it to mean a place for paying tribute or tax - "skat" meaning tax and "vollr", a field, but a very similar placename, "Scatval", exists in Norway where it is thought to derive from the word "scat" in Old Norse meaning "the top of a tree" or "the furthest end of something" and the generic word "val" used for land which has been felled and cleared by burning and some suggest that this is a possible meaning for Scatwell. Whatever the meaning, no evidence for settlement by Norse people has ever been found at Scatwell and it is generally thought that the area of Ross-shire was visited by the Norse people from Sutherland and Caithness for the purpose of exploiting the timber resources only. Many other Norse placenames in the Ross-shire area seem to refer to trees and timber.

Scatwell is first mentioned, together with Strathconon, in a royal charter of land made to the Mackenzies in 1528. Kenneth Mackenzie, second son of Sir Roderick Mackenzie of Coigeach, tutor of Kintail, was the progenitor of the cadet branch of the Mackenzies of Scatwell. Aonghas MacCoinnich has considered the complex history of the Mackenzies of Scatwell in Chapter 5 and it is not proposed to elaborate any further here except to say that in the 1790s the Mackenzies of Scatwell built a new mansion at Pitanochty near Avoch, renaming it Rosehaugh. This was the original Rosehaugh House which, in 1865, was replaced by a much grander mansion built by the tea merchant, James Fletcher, when he bought the lands. James Wemyss Mackenzie (1770 - 1843) succeeded to the title of 5th Baron of Scatwell in 1811, becoming MP for the County of Ross in 1824 and Lord Lieutenant of Ross in 1826. It was probably he who started building at Scatwell, possibly the original Little Scatwell House, before he died in 1843, and it is certainly the case that his son, Sir James John Randoll Mackenzie (1814 - 1884), 6th Baron of Scatwell and Rosehaugh, carried on in a grand fashion, making extensions to the Mains Farm, stables lodges and keepers cottages (Clough, 1996)

Unfortunately no early estate documents, plans or rentals relevant to Scatwell itself could be traced in the Mackenzie of Scatwell papers for the period before 1850 and the earliest detailed evidence for settlement in this area is the Roy map of c1750. Although not very reliable it gave a good idea of the settlements at that time and indicates that there were 12 townships, with the majority of the valley floor occupied by cultivation strips. Interestingly there was only a limited amount of woodland. The only other document that gave information on settlement and population in this period was the 1798 list[1]. Little remains of the early townships, they have been destroyed by subsequent development; the township of Milltown of Scatwell, for example, was replaced by Scatwell House and its policies and all that remains is the mill lade and dam which has been enhanced as part of the garden landscaping. Similarly the township of Little Scatwell was replaced by the first Little Scatwell House, depicted on the 1st edition OS map; a new house has since been built on the same site. At Drumandarach the old township was replaced by a sheep farm and the substantial bank on the north side of the large enclosure is the only visible remains of the original settlement, although it is suspected that the remains of buildings lie underneath some of the larger clearance cairns.

---

[1] NAS GD46-17-80-200-00001

Most of the lower glen is or has been part of the Scatwell estate and there have been many changes over the years, particularly during the 19th century. Comrie, for instance, was part of the estates of Mackenzie of Coul, but is now part of the Little Scatwell estate and Achonachie, today part of the Fairburn Estate, was together with Glen Orrin, part of the Meikle Scatwell estate for a period in the 19th century. From 1831-32 the lands of Scatwell and Lochluichart were broken up and each side of the river sold separately. Meikle Scatwell, on the south side of the river, was sold in 1832 and was to pass to Mrs Stewart Mackenzie of Seaforth c1844. On the north side of the river, Little Scatwell and Lochluichart were still owned by Sir James John Randoll Mackenzie. He was to make many improvements at both Scatwell and Rosehaugh Estates, but his extravagant lifestyle incurred considerable debts and he sold Little Scatwell in 1849 and Kinlochluichart and Glenmarksie in 1853. This made little difference to his debts and he was declared bankrupt in 1864.

# 7. The pre-improvement period - black cattle and the shieling system

The most numerous structures to be found in the mountainous parts of Strathconon during the archaeological recording project were those of shielings. In most of the side glens and beside many mountain streams, groups of between three and 24 grassy mounds, the remains of small oval shieling huts, were found. They represent the pre-improvement period when there was intensive cattle rearing and may be part of an activity which goes back hundreds of years. The cattle of 300 years ago were the forerunners of today's Highland cattle. They were much smaller, hardier, easy to handle and, contrary to general belief, black in colour; the red/brown variety was not introduced until the 19th century when they became popular with the romantic Victorians.

From the early days of the clans until 200 years ago cattle were vital to the survival of the Highlander. Beef, both on the hoof and salted in barrels, was an important source of food. The animals could be bled without killing them, the blood being mixed with oatmeal to make an early version of black pudding. The hides would have been used as bedding or clothing and equally, if not more importantly, the clansman could pay his rent in kind by using cattle. By 1607 free trade had been agreed between England and Scotland and cattle were being exported and driven to the markets of Falkirk and Crieff in the south. After the Union of 1707 there was an upsurge in demand for cattle from Scotland and in the later 18th century, when Britain was involved in a series of overseas conflicts, there was a significant demand from the Navy for salt beef. Cattle were a resource which could be sold giving the Highlander and, indirectly through his rent, his landlord, much needed cash. This shift to cash would have suited the landlords nicely

> One of the stipulations of the States of Iona (1609) was that the sons of Highland chiefs should be educated in the Lowlands. Previously many had been fostered through an arrangement that bred or cemented alliances, with cattle being used as payment. The consequence of this change was that not only were future chiefs and chieftains now exposed to a different code of behaviour but they acquired new tastes, their expectations changed as they became involved with Lowland society and even visits to the continent. They acquired an appetite for fine clothes and furnishings, to judge from some reports their taste for fine living spread to other senior clan members. (Dodgshon, 1998, p115)

And Tom Devine (1994, p43) expresses the view

> If chiefs were becoming an integral part of the British landed elite, they could not remain immune from the material, intellectual and cultural goals of the class. Among the aristocracy and gentry, the 18th century was an era of conspicuous consumption, of ornate and expensive building, foreign travel and a more opulent lifestyle.

Rents paid in cash would have facilitated this lifestyle.

The rentals of 1717 to 1726[1] for the upper part of Strathconon show that the rents were paid in cash and clearly cattle must have been exported in order to procure this cash. The great number of shielings in the upper part of Strathconon also supports the theory

---

[1] NAS E655-25-25-00011, E655-26-11-00001, E655-3-5 and E655-3-4

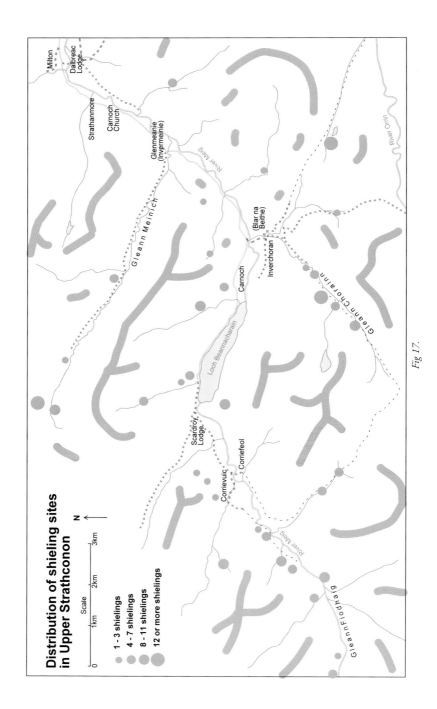

# Distribution of shieling sites in Upper Strathconon

N

Scale

| 0 | 1km | 2km | 3km |

● 1 - 3 shielings
● 4 - 7 shielings
● 8 - 11 shielings
● 12 or more shielings

Milton
Dalbreac Lodge
Strathanmore
Carnoch Church
Glenmeinie (Invermeinie)
River Meig
Gleann Meinich
(Blar na Beithe)
Inverchoran
Carnoch
Gleann Chorainn
Loch Beannacharain
River Orrin
Scardroy Lodge
Corriefeol
Corrievuic
River Meig
Gleann Fiodhaig

Fig 17.

42

*Fig 18.* The remains of the turf and stone walls of a building with rounded corners at Blar na Beithe

that cattle were a major part of the economy. The early rentals for the settlements in the upper part of Strathconon and the list of inhabitants of 1798[2] indicate that the population remained consistently high throughout the 18th century with 15 households paying rent. In addition there may well have been sub tenants paying rent, possibly in kind, to the named tenant. Perhaps 60 or 70 people were living in an area where today there is only the keeper and his wife. It is quite possible that this large population was a legacy from earlier clan days when chiefs needed a large fighting force, although it may also be that, for some reason, there was an overflow of population from Kintail and Lochalsh in the west; Mackenzie chiefs were well known for shifting their tenants around their estates.

The cultivable land in upper Strathconon is extremely limited and the growing period very short: there would have been insufficient grain for the needs of a large population. The cash gained from the export of cattle would have enabled the people to buy grain

> Townships especially those burdened with high tenant numbers or which were less well endowed in resource terms, could ill afford to hand over even part of their grain output as rent especially if arable was scarce or insufficient for those dependent upon it.......By switching rents into cash thereby allowing such tenants to shift their rent burden into less pressurised areas of township economy, notably the livestock sector, land owners effectively gave them a subsistence bonus.......In fact this became a common structural feature of Highland estates for the next two centuries, with the less fertile parts of the estates having cash rents but with grain rents being maintained from the more fertile areas...... The marketing of cattle had two clear advantages; first they were not only a product that could walk to market but also one whose condition could be improved by

[2] NAS GD 46-17-80-201

Lowland feeding and second it enabled the tenant to shift the burden of their rents from what was scarce, or arable, to what was abundant, grass……..not only were chiefs and landowners engaged in marketing cattle themselves, but they would appear to have provided the organisational means by which tenants could market their cattle. In 1641 for instance, the Earl of Seaforth can be found agreeing with an Edinburgh dealer to have 300 cattle delivered by his tenants each year to Stornaway (for export by sea) (Dodgshon, 1998, p110).

The main settlements for the population at this time were the townships. Several tenants occupied a township each family having their own house but sharing resources. A pre-improvement township was made up of a cluster of buildings and adjacent arable land, or "infield", with a kailyard and a few enclosures all surrounded by a head-dyke. Outside the head-dyke the land was held in common and each tenant was entitled to graze his animals there. The houses of this time were smaller than those of later years; they were built of turf or turf and stone and had rounded corners. Today their remains appear as low turf footings which are sometimes difficult to detect having been replaced by larger stone-built houses with squared corners. A few survive in Strathconon and examples of both type of house are found at the townships of Blar-na-Beithe, Corrivuic and Corriefeol.

*Fig 19.* Plan of Blar-na-Beithe, with small cluster of early turf buildings bottom right

An important structure of a township at this time was the kiln for drying grain; an essential requirement in the damp climate of the Highlands. Corn drying kilns consisted of a stone lined pit covered with a grid on which the grain was laid; warm air from an adjacent fire was drawn up through the grid thus drying the grain. The remains of corn drying kilns are seen at both Blar-na-Beithe and Corriefeol and also at Scardroy. Lower down the glen, at Scatwell, there is a fine kiln with attached barns, but this structure may well have had other uses such as making lime or malting grain for whisky!

*Fig 20.* Corn drying kiln at Kinlochbeannacharain/Scardroy

*Fig 21.* Kiln and buildings in woodland above the Allt Dubh, near Scatwell, with plan below

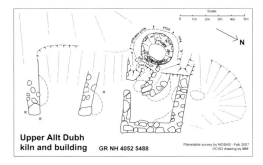

In Strathconon, as with many other glens, most of the remains of the pre-improvement townships of the 18th century have disappeared but those of their summer sheiling grounds have not. The practice known as transhumance or the removal of people and their animals to mountain pastures in the summertime was essential to a cattle economy. Once people settled down to grow crops it was necessary to move the livestock, which may have included sheep and goats as well as the cattle, well away from the townships. The fresh mountain pastures in the upper glens became an essential part of rural life with the people and their animals staying at their shielings for months at a time. In late May or early June the women and children would make their way to the shielings grounds with the cattle. The adult men of the township would have made ready the huts for occupation, but they would return to the townships to tend the growing crops and repair the winter houses. The women and children would remain at the shielings producing butter and cheese until August. Dairy produce formed a large element of the people's rental payment in kind. During these summer months there was a constant two way traffic between the shielings and the parent township, transferring produce and supplies. Many of the well trodden shieling tracks are still in use today.

*Fig 22.* A shieling mound, one of six at Corrie Bhuic

As with the township buildings, the early shieling huts were constructed of turf or turf and stone and the later ones were built entirely of stone. The two types of construction at a site may suggest that the site has been in use for a long period of time. Shieling huts are often found in clusters and it may be that some protection against cattle rustling was afforded by the larger number of people. All aspects of human life went on at shielings; children were born, people became ill or died and support from each other was of great importance. In the Highlands transhumance came to an end in the late 18th Century, but in the Hebrides the practice did not die out until the early 20th Century.

*Fig 23.* A shieling mound, one of ten at Coille Innis na Sine

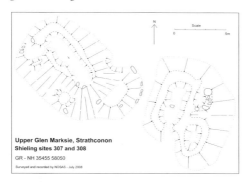

**Upper Glen Marksie, Strathconon**
**Shieling sites 307 and 308**

GR - NH 35455 58050

Surveyed and recorded by NOSAS - July 2008

*Fig 24.* NOSAS members surveying two shieling huts in upper Glen Marksie, with the plan above

Three hundred shielings were recorded in the whole of Strathconon during the NOSAS project and more may have been missed. Clusters of the small turf buildings were located throughout the upper glen on every favourable bit of ground besides a burn. At Loch Airigh Lochain to the east of Inverchoran, for instance, there is a large grassy piece of ground with a dozen shieling mounds; the very name is a give-away, the element "airigh" translates as "shieling" in Gaelic. In Corrie Bhuic there are several large grassy mounds within an area of extensive heathery ground.

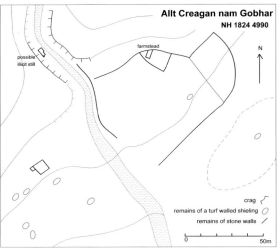

*Fig 25.* Plan of the shieling site at Allt Creagan nam Gobhar, note the more recent farmstead, enclosures and a possible illicit still bothy

Further down the glen, at the head of Glen Meinich, there are two groups of shielings; one, centred on NH 2222 5545, has 19 huts and the other, at NH 2218 5522, has 11. In Glenmarksie, at NH 3544 5798, there are 24 shielings some with integral cells or stores. At most of the sites the structures appear to be of the earlier type - oval grassy mounds with dished centres sometimes as much as one metre in height, but at several sites, in Gleann Chorain for example, stone walled shielings of later date were recorded. At many of the sites there is evidence of more permanent settlement; two shieling sites, 3 kilometres to the SW of Corrievuic, have farmsteads and enclosures; the grassy mounds of the shieling huts are however still very obvious. One of these sites is on the south side of the river below Coille Innis na Sine and the other is on the north side of the river to the east of Creag na h-Iolaire, around the Allt Creagan nam Gobhar (not marked on current OS map). Several still bothies were found in the vicinity of the shieling sites - it is quite possible that the people carried on their illicit business while tending their animals – a good alibi! and the by-products of distillation, draff and pot ale, would have been nutritious feed stuffs for young stock.

Most of the shielings were within easy reach of their parent township but in a few cases the shieling grounds could be at a great distance. There may, for example, have been shielings in the upper reaches of Glen Orrin to the south or there may have been some overlap with other settlements

In 1667 the lands of Comrie and Tarvie had their grazings in Glennuiak (Gleann Fhiodag, NH 110 479) in the upper reaches of the River Meig (Comrie and Tarvie, near Scatwell, are nearly 20 miles from Gleann Fhiodaig) (MacCoinnich, 2009).

Some shieling grounds were placed strategically on estate boundaries and estate owners ensured their occupation to prevent trespass by tenants of neighbouring estates. One example of this practice was located in the documents, although this example was aimed at preventing intrusion of the Strathconon people into neighbouring estates

> These days we might consider the remote hills as a wasteland or wilderness, but several hundred years ago they were keenly contested, not just for their potential as hunting and fishing grounds but also their value as summer grazing. They were jealously guarded. Mr James Fraser, writer of the Wardlaw manuscripts (1660) informs us that the Tutor of Lovat at Beauly in 1589 gave the lands of Ardnagrask to Donald and John MacIver in order that they might keep the marches along the River Orrin, between Ardnacrask and Coire Chaibre, secure "against the Stratchounin men" (MacCoinnich, 2009)

MacCoinnich in Chapter 5 (pp33-34) concludes, from the documentary evidence, that cattle production was the main focus of activity and the mainstay of the economy in Strathconon, suggesting that this emphasis on cattle farming on marginal lands closely paralleled what was happening elsewhere in Highland Scotland during this period.

## Cattle Reiving

The reiving or thieving of the cattle of other clans was an age old tradition of clan warriors in the Scottish Highlands and had been going on for centuries. In some respects it was as much a sport where clan warriors, keen to show their skill and judgment, descended from the hills to carry off their neighbour's stock. Strathconon, a crucial through route, was to experience its share of cattle reivers in the later years, although the clansmen who returned to the ways of cattle raiding in the late 17th and 18th century did so in order to survive and were in fact Jacobites, fighting a doomed guerilla campaign and struggling against a government army that had a garrison in practically every glen. JH Dixon relates a tale of cattle raiding, which figures Scardroy, in the late 17th Century (Dixon, 1886, p50)

> Iain Geal Donn, a noted cattle-lifter from Lochaber, came with his men to An Amilt in Easter Ross and there lifted eleven cows and a bull. They came with their spoil through Strath Vaich and Strathconan to a place called Sgaird Ruadh or Scardroy where they stayed the night. It was they who gave the name to this place because they had pushed the beasts so hard that blood came from them. Alastair Buidhe Mackay (employed by the laird of Gairloch at the time to help repel cattle thieves) had a Lochaber lad for a servant and it was this lad who told him that the thieves were stopping that night at the sheiling bothie at Scardroy. Mackay and his servant hurried away to Scardroy and there he made the lad swear to be faithful to him and not let any of the thieves come out alive. The thieves were in the bothie, quite unsuspicious and roasting a portion of bull. Mackay posted his servant at the door whilst he himself climbed on the other end of the bothie. He quietly lifted the lower edge of a divot of the roof and peeped in to see what was going on. He saw Iain Geal Donn looking very jolly and warming the backs of the calves of his legs at the fire. Iain suddenly turned round and said to his men who were about the fire roasting the meat "Look out! I am getting the smell of powder"

Before he could say another word there was a charge from Mackay's gun. The instant he had fired the shot Mackay rushed to the door to assist his servant and the two of them shot all the Lochaber men but one who escaped. Mackay and his lad ate their fill of the meat before returning to Gairloch to tell the laird of their success. A running ghillie was sent to Brahan with a letter to tell Lord Mackenzie of Kintail who at the time was dining with Cameron of Locheil. After the reading the letter his Lordship threw it over to Locheil saying "There is blood on you over there, you thieves" Locheil was so stung that he left the dinner untouched and went straight home to Lochaber. He sent ghillies to Scardroy and they brought away the body of Iain Geal Donn. They buried him in Corpach, Lochaber where his memorial cairn stands to this day

Jacobite reivers, destitute after the "scorched earth" policy of the government following the Battle of Culloden, were often from Lochaber. A document dated 6th Aug 1746 has[3]

A letter from Captain George Munro [of Culcairn] 'Commanding a Detachment of His Majesties Forces in Lochbroom', to Sergeant Finlay Munro of Captain Munro's Independent Company orders Finlay Munro to march with a party of the troop to Kinlochewe, Strathbrenn (Strathbran), Strathconan, Strathgarve and the parishes of Lochcarron, Lochalsh and Kintail searching for livestock stolen from parish of Roskeen or Kincarden. These and 'Any other effects, stolen out of this country at the tyme of the late unnatural rebellion' are to be seized and returned to their true owners and those who have them unlawfully in their possession are to be 'sent to proper goalls(sic) to underly the law, for their theft and rebellion'

## Cattle Droving

The skills required for cattle rustling and caring for cattle on the move were also those which were required for droving. The reivers of one century were to become the legitimate drovers of the next. By the middle of the 17th century the droving trade had grown to a huge operation and many opportunities had arisen for drovers. In 1663, 18,574 cattle were recorded as passing through Carlisle on the border between Scotland and England. Cattle prices had quadrupled and total exports of cattle from Scotland had quintupled in the course of the 18th century (Devine, 1994, p42).

The drovers were mostly Highlanders; to the southerners with whom they dealt, they were: 'great, stalwart, hirsute men'; 'shaggy, uncultured and wild'; 'dressed usually in homespun tweeds which smelt of heather and peat smoke'. In Strathconon there is evidence of two such, Alexander Macdonald of Invermeinie from the 1798 list[4] and Duncan MacIver of Blarnabee (Blar-na-Beithe) from the 1841 census. In May, they would start to visit farms and bargain for cattle. Many of the Highland farming tenants were poor and may only have had one or two beasts at a time to sell. Gradually, the drover would gather together a herd of at least 100, often larger and sometimes up to 2,000 cattle. Ahead of them lay a long and dangerous journey. Rivers in flood might have to be crossed; journeys made over trackless mountains, sometimes in thick mist where the route might easily be lost. The drover had to know where he could obtain enough grazing. At day's end, the cattle might stop near a rough inn where some shelter

[3] NAS GD1-1030-24
[4] NAS GD 46-17-80-201

could be obtained, or perhaps the drovers had to sleep out in the open with only their woven cloth plaid to protect them. At night someone had to be on guard to prevent cattle straying or reivers stealing them. It was a hard and, at times, dangerous life, but the Highlanders, with their warlike past, and hardy upbringing were well suited to it. The drovers would sell their cattle at the Falkirk or Crieff Trysts to others who moved them on to grazing areas in Northumberland or the Yorkshire Dales in northern England where they would be fattened up before the final journey to London and the south.

Undoubtedly Strathconon would have seen a good number of droves. It was on the route from Poolewe on the west coast (where the cattle from the Isle of Lewis were landed) to the east and south and later to Muir of Ord where there was a market. The droves almost certainly travelled via the inn at Badinluchie, in Strathbran, and perhaps they passed through Glenmarksie making their way to Scatwell where there was another inn. The linear turf banks and stone enclosures in the trees to the west of Glenmarksie Lodge may be evidence of the droves passing through.

For over two hundred years, from the early seventeenth century to the early nineteenth century, droving flourished and was aided by a growing human population. The peace after the battle of Waterloo in 1815 and the discharge of many of the soldiers meant that the demand for beef declined. Faster steamships provided an easier alternative to the long arduous overland droves. By 1880 railways provided an even swifter and more reliable means of transporting cattle and droving gradually died out.

**Strathconon on the eve of Improvement**
The Old Statistical Account for the parish of Contin states that in 1791 cattle were still a substantial part of the economy.

> There is not an inclosure in the parish, the people are averse to inclosures as they wish to have all kinds of pasture in common. The situation of 1782 and 1783 was truly deplorable and no doubt many of the poorer sort must have died from want, were it not for the timely supply of corn sent by the government. One remarkable circumstance to be observed was that although these years produced little or no corn they were particularly favourable for the growth of grass which yielded immense quantities of milk, the principal support of the inhabitants. Another favourable circumstance was that there was a great demand for cattle, the staple commodity of the parish, and they sold at a high price.........the population is on the increase but is feared will soon decrease as the gentlemen are encouraging shepherds to come and settle on their properties which must necessarily remove the present inhabitants and force them to go in quest of bread to other countries as there are no manufactures established here to employ them (Mackenzie, 1791)

The much respected agriculturalist Sir John Sinclair writes about cattle and the life of the people in the central glens of Ross-shire in 1795 and offers some suggestions for "Improvement"

> The interior parts of Ross-shire are justly described as an extensive and beautiful Highland country, the straths or valleys are rich and fertile whilst the hills produce

abundant grass for feeding cattle, horses sheep and goats. Till of late this district was inhabited by a number of small farmers who maintained themselves and their families from the produce of the little spots they had to cultivate and who in favourable seasons were enabled to pay the trifling rent exacted by the landlord from the profit of the cattle they possessed. The indolence which they indulged themselves in, the abundance of fuel they enjoyed and the natural attachment which every individual must feel for his native soil and birth place made them attached to the mode of living and unwilling to quit it. In a public view it was a matter of considerable importance to have a brave and hardy race of men kept in the country who without much detriment to agriculture or to commerce industry could at once be converted to soldiers. But of late a change of system has taken place. This extensive district is rapidly being converted from cattle into sheep farms, and there is no doubt of its being infinitely better for the latter. For every pound of beef that a Highlander can send to market a shepherd can at least bring three pound of mutton. Hence the shepherd is enabled to pay as much as double the rent with ease and it can hardly be questioned that in the process of time a Highland property would be tripled or quadrupled in value by sheep farming......
There seems to be no difficulty in forming a plan by which the natives of the country might convert their stock of cattle into sheep, equally to their own, their landlords and the public advantage......Let all the Highlands west of Contin be divided into townships with a sufficient quantity of hill and dale for an extensive sheepfarm annexed to each......Let the proprietor make choice of four or five of his most substantial tenants to be settled on every township of £100 rent. Let them have lease for 21 years on condition of their purchasing a stock of sheep and selling off all their horses, cattle and goats except two cows and one horse for each family; the latter for the purpose of ploughing their small spots of arable ground, of carrying home their peat or turf and bringing meal or grain from the low country......it would certainly be worthwhile for Col Mackenzie of Seaforth, Sir Hector Mackenzie of Gairloch, Mr Mackenzie of Applecross and other proprietors of Highland estates, not only in the county of Ross but in the rest of Scotland (Sinclair, 1795)

It was inevitable that sheep would come to the Highlands. These were times of change and the future was unknown. Sir John's solution was to be put into practice by the Earl of Seaforth but proved not to be the answer; the old tenants were not easily converted to sheep farming. By the 1830s all the tacks in Strathconon were large sheep farms with single tenants. For a while cattle continued to be part of the Highland economy but on a much smaller scale

The few black cattle reared for sale are the remains of the old Highland breed which seem to have degenerated in the same ratio in which the circumstances of the people have declined (Downie, 1837)

# 8. Improvement and sheep farming

In the late 18th century, landowners became much more commercialized and, believing that sheep-rearing was one of the most effective ways of improving and exploiting their lands, they began to introduce sheep to the Highlands on a large scale. This conversion to sheep farming was encouraged by fairly steady growth in the demand for wool with a further increase during the Napoleonic War years of 1790 to 1815. The price of wool and sheep multiplied. Sheep farmers competed for land at high rents and there was a trend towards longer leases. Tom Devine writes

> Overseas supply of woollen manufactures from Europe was limited and erratic during the Napoleonic Wars and it was only when Australia started to export in volume in 1820 that it picked up. In the interim the gap was increasingly filled by Highland sheep farmers (Devine, 1994, p42)

Sheepfarming and "Improvement" came relatively late to Strathconon. In 1802 several tacks of land in Strathconon were advertised to let as sheep farms. James Hogg, the Ettrick shepherd, was one who visited the glen with a mind to taking a tack, he writes

> Amongst the fellow lodgers (he was staying at an inn on Rannoch Moor), I was glad at meeting here with Mr McCallum, who had taken an extensive farm on the estate of Strathconnon, which I viewed last year, he informed me that all that extensive estate was let to sheep farmers (Hogg, 1888)

There is documentary evidence to suggest that Lord Seaforth deferred the introduction of sheep to his west coast estates because he had promised land and reduced rents to returning men from the military operations overseas and it is highly probable that the

*Fig 26.* The remains of the farmstead and sheep enclosures at Doirevaire in the upper glen

same applied to Strathconon. At the time the estate was administered by trustees for the Earl of Seaforth, with Brigadier (later General Sir) Alexander Mackenzie of Fairburn at the helm. Fairburn was to have a distinguished military career in the 78th Highlanders serving in many parts of the world. He divided the glen into seven sheepwalks, five being rented by multiple or club tenants from the old tenantry and two by incoming sheep farmers[1]. The greater number of multiple tenancies reflects Seaforth's policies on other parts of his estates and indicates his promise to accommodate his former tenants.

Many tacks in the Highlands were let to incomers with sheep farming experience from the Lowlands and the Borders and certainly this is the case in Strathconon. Later, Armstrong from Roxburgh and Cunningham from Douglas, near Lanark, are noted in the census' of 1841 and 1851. But in the earlier period some Highlanders had key roles in the rapid economic and social changes associated with sheep farming. In 1803 responsibility for two tacks in Strathconon was taken on by Alexander Macdonald of Glencoe and Adam Macdonald of Achtriachtan (also in Glencoe). Adam Macdonald had inherited Achtriachtan from his father but in the opinion of Charles Fraser Mackintosh, WS, solicitor in Inverness, he was

> quite unfit to manage his patrimonial estate……..Through his close connections with Alexander Macdonald of Glencoe he doubtless imbibed the idea of making his fortune by sheep farming. He lost frightfully by becoming a tenant or liable for sub-tenants of large farms in Strathconon………a debt arising from his cautionary obligations into which he had been artfully inveigled (Fraser Mackintosh, 1898)

Alexander Macdonald and Adam Macdonald became entangled in a complicated arrangement concerning lands in Strathconon. Both acted as cautioners, or guarantors, for two sheep farmers who wished to rent land in the glen using their lands in Glencoe as security. Alexander Macdonald for Donald McBarnett of Lochaber, who was interested in Glenmarksie, which at the time was owned by William Mackenzie of Strathgarve, and Adam Macdonald for James MacCallum who wished to rent Dalbreac.

The two tacks let as single tenancies in Strathconon are of concern here, the five tacks let to existing tenants are explored in Chapter 9. Iain Macdonald (2005, p162) tells us

> In 1803 he (Mackenzie of Fairburn) let the glen out in seven tacks, mostly for 19 years, but in one case, 21 years. He gave five tacks in the upper reaches of Strathconon to his former tenants who were already there or who held ground in the lower part of Strathconon which they had to leave. This made the lower ground available as two extensive tacks for new tenants. In each tack it was said that the ground was given "for the purpose of covering the same with sheep, houses biggings and yards……The lower of the two extensive new tacks consisted of three farms; Glacour, Annate and Easter Balnault, this went to John Cameron and John MacLaren from Glenalmond for 19 years at a rent of £150. The other tack, for which Adam Macdonald of Achtriachtan was "cautioner, security and full debtor", was an even larger one and consisted of "the whole of the townlands and grazings of Inverchoran, Blarnabee, Balnacreig and that part of the land lying

---

[1] NAS RD2-293-00 p164- 178

to the south of the Water of Conon, Cranich, Knockdhu, Dalbreck, Wester Balnault with the grazings of Luiblone and Corrienaslevich (in Glen Orrin). This was given to "John MacCallum and Duncan MacCallum his son" for 21 years from 1803 at a rent of £450 per annum.......The farms listed in this tack extended for several miles along the south side of the river, south across the watershed to the River Orrin and west to touch the west end of Loch Monar. Subsequent events are rather obscure. It was said many years later that the MacCallums were removed by Adam Macdonald and replaced by tenants of his own choosing. This suggests that the MacCallums had failed and left Adam Macdonald, as cautioner, with responsibility for the whole tack. Adam Macdonald's chaotic state of affairs led, in 1816, to the appointment of interdictors and trustees. In a rental of 1819 an entry is made for "Achtriachtans Farms in Ross-shire" and Donald, John and Allan Macdonald, brothers of the Innerigan family (also of Glencoe) were described as tenants of Dalnabreck but they too failed. An advertisement appeared in the Inverness Courier, 28 Dec 1820 "for the sale of the whole stock of sheep, black cattle and horses belonging to the sequestered estate of Donald Macdonald upon the farms of Monar and Dalbreck" and a summons for his removal from Dalbreck was presented early in 1821.

The low turf and stone footings of a farmstead are seen on the south side of the track between Dalbreac Lodge and Mains of Dalbreac, this may have been the early sheep farm of the MacCallums. In September 1818 James MacCallum gave evidence at a court case when three individuals were indicted for deforcing and assaulting officers of the revenue. The three, along with several others, had been illegally distilling whisky at a site probably in Glen Meinich. Two Excise officers had left MacCallum's house on horseback in the morning in perfect health and returned the same day, one with head injuries and severe bruising. MacCallum dressed the injuries, gave them a bed for the night and sent his son to see them safely down the glen the next morning[2].

Of the second tack under Fairburn's supervision, that of Glacour, Annate and Easter Balnault let to James Cameron and John MacLaren, little is known. The lessees appear to have moved on before the end of their lease as an advertisement appears in the *Inverness Journal* in January 1812 for "the farms of Easter Balnault, Annate and Glackour with valuable grazing to let, lately possessed by James Cameron and John McLaren". The remains of a farmstead and sheepfold are bisected by the present road at Balnault - was this the farm that they occupied?

Alexander Macdonald of Glencoe, in his dealings with Glenmarksie, fared little better than Adam Macdonald. Donald MacBarnett, for whom Glencoe was cautioner, paid his rent for one year and then made no further payments for two years. Glencoe was responsible for paying the £295 in arrears, which he did but the money never reached Mackenzie of Strathgarve. Glencoe died in 1816 and in 1821 his trustees pursued the £295 through the courts but without success. From 1810 Alexander Macdonald let Glenmarksie to a series of tenants and sub-tenants but it was always to remain a problem for him and eventually in 1821 an early exit to the lease arrangements was

2 Inverness Journal, April 23, 1819

*Fig 27.* Farmstead at Soulmarksie in the lower glen, with plan below

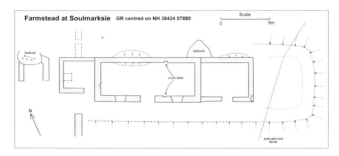

negotiated. By this time however a significant loss had been made by Glencoe and his trustees (Macdonald, 2005, p168-169).

The high rents and long leases proved disastrous for all the sheep farming entrepreneurs in Strathconon. By 1821 some of the multiple tenancies of the old tenantry had also failed, Carnoch and Glenmeinich had been taken over probably in 1808 by a single tenant, possibly Earl O'Neil who is named in a rental of 1819[3]. One source quotes his purpose as being "for shooting"[4], although it is probable that he was non-resident and that he sub-let the tack to several of the original tenants.

Sheep farming in Strathconon appears to have gone through a bleak period in the 1820s. Seaforth died in 1815 and his daughter, Mary Elizabeth Frederica had inherited the estate. In 1817 she married James Alexander Stewart of Glasserton and the couple took the surname Stewart-Mackenzie. When the tacks in Strathconon came up for

[3] NAS GD46-17-80-248-0001
[4] NAS GD46-17-59-00001

renewal in 1822, the whole estate was advertised for sale[5]. Presumably a buyer was not found for it was still in the hands of Mrs Stewart-Mackenzie in 1833 when it was advertised again. A buyer was not found until 1839 when it became the property of Mr James Balfour of Whittingham. Fairburn continued in his role as head of the trustees until 1821, but appears to have given up shortly afterwards. It is known that he sold his own estate of Fairburn and moved to London at some point.

During this time the demand for wool remained high, in 1828 Scottish wool accounted for 10% of UK output and by the early 1840s this had risen to 25%. In 1837 the New Statistical Account for Contin Parish states

Several farms are stocked both with Cheviot and black faced sheep and those reared on some grazings fetch the highest prices at market (Downie, 1837)

The years between 1831 and 1833 were a time of change with several advertisements of farms to let in Strathconon. There seems to have been a more ruthless attitude, with tacks for larger sheep farms let at increased rents. From 1834 to 1844 Colin Munro Esq. was paying rent of £410 for Achness, Corriefeol, Scardroy and Carnoch and £100 for Inverchoran[6]. There is little doubt that he could not farm the whole of this area himself and probably sub-let it to shepherds. It is evident that in creating the larger farms tenants were reorganized so that they coexisted beside the sheep in congested communities, each one possessing a smaller piece of land. Hogg's statement in 1803 hints at some dispersal of the population at this time but the numbers remained high; in 1829 it was reported as being 1100. Many people were to leave in the early 1830s, by 1834 the population was 870 and by 1839 it was 568[7].

The estate was sold in 1839 to James Balfour of Whittingham, East Lothian. He continued the process of improvement in Strathconon, leasing farms for sheep but at the same time developing the deer forest. In 1841 he cleared sheep from portions of the ground and, following a reorganization and reduction of the population in 1850, the deer forest was extended. Shooting rents were to be an important element of the estate income.

The 1850s was another period of change for sheep farming and the population. By this time the estate was in the ownership of James Maitland Balfour, the son of Sir James Balfour. James Maitland was to make many improvements and alterations in his short tenure of the estate before his early death at the age of 36 in 1856. The destitution of the large population in the glen had been a constant problem for many years and was brought to a peak in 1846 with the potato famine. A comprehensive plan to improve the situation was embarked upon and is detailed in Chapter 9. It resulted in the reduction of the population and larger sheep farms at Glacour and Achlorachan. Sheep farming continued to be the mainstay for the people of this part of the glen; in the 1881 census sheep farmers are recorded at Balnault, Glacour, Achlorachan and Drumanreach.

A considerable amount of evidence of sheep farming was encountered in the survey project. Many sheepfolds were recorded, some large and stone built, others small and of turf, some rectangular and some circular. Farmsteads, enclosures, sheep dips and

[5] NAS GD46-17-80-248-0003
[6] NAS GD433-1-108 Strathconon Rental 1839
[7] Evidence of James Smith to the Royal Commission 1892

boundary walls were seen throughout the glen. The early sheep farm at Dalbreac, with its low turf footings, has already been mentioned, as has the sheep farm at Drumandarroch in the lower glen, the farmstead and enclosure in Gleann Meinich, known as Callums Croft, was a sheep farm and appears to have been occupied until relatively recently but at Strathanmore the sheep farm has been reduced to a platform only, nothing now exists to suggest a building. Sheep farming also moved into marginal land, extending to more remote parts of the glen and taking over former shieling grounds, as at Doirevaire and Corbae (Coire Beithe) in the upper glen.

*Fig 28.* An irregular enclosure in a sheltered position in the upper glen

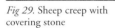

*Fig 29.* Sheep creep with covering stone

*Fig 30.* Sheepfold at Comrie

# 9. Survival, migration and the fate of a large population

The latter part of the 18th century saw a significant increase in population in the Highlands, a trend that was experienced throughout Europe. In 1791 the Old Statistical Account for the parish of Contin states

> The population is on the increase but it is feared will soon decrease as the gentlemen are encouraging shepherds to come and settle on their properties which must necessarily remove the present inhabitants and force them to go in quest of bread, as there is no manufactures established here to employ them (Mackenzie, 1791)

Allan MacInnes (1996) writes

> Population growth put increased pressure on cultivatable areas and profits from droving facilitated permanent movement to shielings……..In the 1790s rising population levels led to congestion within surviving multiple tenancies where the high yields from marginal land afforded by the potato led to the abandonment of customary strip farming in rigs in favour of individual small holdings consolidated as crofting communities

The high population in Strathconon has already been mentioned. This population was to be subjected to greater pressure at the turn of the century. Landlords, looking for ways to make their estates give them a better return, were introducing sheep farming. But there was a dilemma: sheep farming, if it were to be done profitably, required letting tacks as single tenancies to incoming farmers with experience; how could the existing tenantry be accommodated? Some landlords removed people to crofting communities on the coast where they were expected to make a living with a combination of farming and fishing, others were to establish industries such as weaving, quarrying or mining, but many landlords were to send their people away from the glens.

The Earl of Seaforth saw himself as the patriarch of Clan Mackenzie; he had recruited a significant number of tenants to his regiments, promising them land in return for military service. He was unwilling and unable to remove his small tenants to make way for large sheep farms. He retained multiple-tenancy farms in order to accommodate his former clansmen when it was generally recognized that the way forward for sheep farming was by letting tacks as single tenancies.

With the coming of the improvement period the physical nature of the old townships was to change. Some of the original practices continued; the arable land for instance continued to be cultivated in strips on the "in-field" (although this was to change with the later introduction of the potato) and cattle, sheep and goats were grazed on the common ground. Almost certainly the old turf houses would have continued in use as byres or stores, but the emphasis was on improvement of all aspects of farming, whether it be introduction of sheep, more efficient methods of agriculture, new crops or improved housing. The turf built houses were to be replaced by more substantial stone built buildings which were reckoned to be healthier and more suitable. Some landlords insisted on these new houses, laying down specifications in the tacks they gave their tenants. One of the conditions of the multiple tenancy tacks of Strathconon given in 1803 was[1]

---

[1] NAS RD2-293-00164

It is hereby agreed that all the houses on the towns and lands hereby let are to be (?) assessed by two or more skilfull persons mutually chosen and that the tenants shall be allowed meleration for whatever substantial houses they should build to the extent of £100 ……. provided the dwelling houses are built of stone and mortar, finished with lime and the side walls thereof be at least six feet high with suitable office houses partly stone and partly walling

*Fig 31.* The remains of the stone walls of a building with squared corners at Clach Loundrain

*Fig 32.* A dwelling house at Strathanmore c.1870, no evidence of the house exists today.
Photograph reproduced by kind permission of AM Brander

*Fig 34.* Cruck slots were noted in several buildings in Strathconon, this one at Soulmarksie

*Fig 33.* Cruck frames support the roof of this barn in the Borders. Crown Copyright RCAHMS. Licensor www.rcahms.gov.uk

The township at Invermeinie, GR NH 284526, located in the angle between two rivers, has the remains of a very substantial building, the walls are 2m thick and up to 0.8m high in places. It is well constructed with three large compartments and has the feel of being "estate built", yet the inhabitants had lived the lives of the older townships; there was at least one corn-drying kiln and 19 storage pits, probably for potatoes. It is thought that this building dates from 1803 when Mackenzie of Fairburn issued the multiple tenancy tack and gave the specifications for the buildings above – three tenants from Balnault in the lower glen were settled here alongside the six existing tenants.

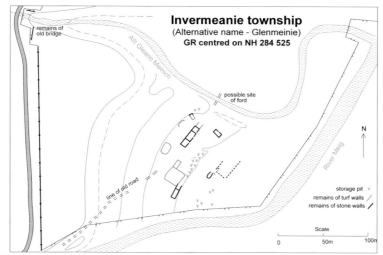

*Fig 35.* Plan of the settlement at Glenmeinie, sometimes known as Invermeinie or Invervannie

61

The remains of deserted townships and farmsteads are much more evident in the upper glen. Six settlements, two of them with corn-drying kilns are seen in the vicinity of Scardroy and Corrievuic, others lower down the glen are at Blar-na-Beithe, near Inverchoran, Carnoch, Invermeinie and in the middle part of Glen Meinich. In the lower glen the townships of Little Scatwell and Milton of Scatwell have disappeared completely, replaced by Little Scatwell House and Scatwell House. Drumandarroch and Comrie have seen so much sheep farming activity that the former townships have disappeared and at Coulintore, beside Loch Achonachie, the township has been planted with trees. The township of Achonachie itself has been submerged by the loch and further west the settlements of Balnault and Drumanriach too have been inundated by Loch Meig.

The introduction of sheep and "Improvement" came relatively late to Strathconon. The glen was administered by trustees with Brigadier (later General Sir) Alexander Mackenzie of Fairburn playing an important role. Some landlords had placed their estates in the hands of trustees in order for them to pursue their political careers. That may well have been the case with Strathconon, but the transfer to trustees is more likely to have been associated with the parlous state of the Seaforth finances. Nevertheless in these situations clear guidelines for the management of the estates, the collection of rents and renewal of leases were usually given by the landowner.

In 1803 Mackenzie of Fairburn divided Strathconon into seven tacks, five being let to multiple or club tenants from the old tenantry and two to incoming sheep farmers mostly for 19 years but in one case 21 years. Fairburn had previous experience of the management of the Seaforth estates as one of the advisers to the Earl when, in 1801, a sale of Kintail, one of the west coast properties, was considered. The arrangement in Strathconon in 1803 was very similar to that on the west coast estate of Glensheal in 1801, five tacks in the upper reaches of Strathconon were given to former tenants who were already there or who had held ground in the lower part of Strathconon which they had to leave to make way for the two extensive tacks for incoming sheep farmers. The five tacks going to the multiple tenants laid down several conditions beside that already mentioned for building stone houses[2]

> in case the rent shall at any time continue in arrears for three months, it is hereby agreed that it shall be in the power of the said Brigadier General Alexander Mackenzie to remove the said tenants before named at the next term of Whitsunday…….. It is hereby agreed that each one of the tenants shall grind all the grindable corn at the miln of Strathconon and pay the accustomed multures and miln dues for the same and perform the accustomed services thereat

There seems to be no doubt that Fairburn had experienced the hostility of club farm tenants in letting tacks for sheep to incomers. One of the additional conditions of the tacks going to the former tenants was

> Whereas the said Brigadier General Alexander Mackenzie has introduced strangers as sheep farmers into the country of Strathconon with which measure the country people do not seem to be well affected. It is hereby specially provided and declared that if any of the tenants before named… or any person in their

[2] NAS RD2-293-00164

employment shall give said strangers tenants or any of them any molestations of trouble… and that they or any of them shall be convicted of the same by any competent judge… these presents shall become void.

In 1802 James Hogg, the Ettrick shepherd, visited the glen with a mind to taking a tack
Amongst the fellow lodgers (he was staying at an inn on Rannoch Moor), I was glad at meeting here with Mr McCallum, who had taken an extensive farm on the estate of Strathconnon, which I viewed last year. He informed me that all that extensive estate was let to sheep farmers saving a small division on the lower end, which the General had reserved for the accommodation of such of the natives as could not dispose of themselves to better advantage (Hogg, 1888)

That part in the lower glen was probably Curin, the *Inverness Courier* reports on 15th August, 1850 in an article "The State of Strathconon"
The Campbells applied to Mr Balfour for liberty to build a house at Curin, a small detached part of the property at the east end where several cottars sit rent free, the spot having been set aside for that purpose.

A rental of 1819[3] gives some idea of the extent of the five multiple tenancies let in 1803. In most of the tacks the tenant named has been identified on the 1798 list[4]
1. Corriefeol, Corrievuich, Achiness and Backlinan were possessed by "Kenneth McCrae and others" paying £300 (a Kenneth Macrae appears in "Corbuie" in the 1798 list)
2. Keanlochbeanchran was in the hands of Duncan MacGregor and others paying £180 (Murdoch Macgregor and his two sons Murdoch and Duncan all appear as tenants in Scardroy on the 1798 list)
3. Invervenie and Carnoch were in the possession of Earl O'Neil paying £367, but they had originally been let in 1803 as a multiple tenancies. An advertisement in the *Inverness Journal* on 20 May, 1808 indicates that the multiple tenancies had failed by this time
To be let - the lands and grazings of Carnoch and Inverveiny, with appendages as presently possessed by the tenants thereof. They will answer for either the grazing of black cattle or as a sheep farm
These lands are again advertised to let in 1812 and 1819. A letter of 1822[5] states that the lands were let to Lord O'Neil for shooting, but that he was subletting them.
4. Balblair and Drumfearn were in the possession of "Donald Beton and others" paying £80 (a Donald Bethune appears as tenant in Drumfearn in the 1798 list)

Why did the Inverveinie and Carnoch tacks fail? The ethos of a club-farm was that the joint tenants were equally responsible for the rent. It was a system that had been common in previous years and seemed to work well when cattle was the main stock, but with the movement towards improvement and sheep farming the original tenants were at a disadvantage and the conditions for discord were increased. Many people did not have experience of sheep farming or the capital to invest in stock, some perhaps were unwilling or unable to co-operate with the rest of the group in improving the stock and

[3] NAS GD46-17-80-248-0001
[4] NAS GD46-17-80-200-0001
[5] NAS GD46-17-80-248-0001

the land. It may have been a combination of these and several other factors that led to the failure at Inverveinie and Carnoch. In addition, when establishing the multiple tenancy of Inverveinie in 1803, the tack had been given to nine tenants, six of whom were former tenants and three who were removed from West Balnault (originally close to Bridgend) to make way for the sheepfarm of Dalbreac[6] – it is quite possible that there was discord and disagreement between the two factions.

Somers (1847) writes about the imperfections of the club farm tenancies in Lochcarron, another former Seaforth possession

> The club-tenants are everywhere a much more substantial class than the crofters, their stock forming a resource on which they can fall back in a period of calamity. But it needs but a single glance at their system of farming to see that they are far from being so comfortable as their means and opportunities might make them. Their great objective is to wring as much corn crop from their farm as possible by which they expect two advantages – oatmeal for their families and straw for the cattle during the winter. But everybody knows that cows cannot milk well if fed upon dry straw and as they are kept roaming over hill for pasture during a great part of the year their manure is also lost. Their crops are frequently so poor as to yield little more than seed......In these Highland townships there are two conflicting parties at work – the party of the old men and the party of the young men; in the agricultural sense the former are conservative while the latter are revolutionary. The old men cling rigidly to the old system of cattle rearing wheras the young men are for diminishing the number of cattle and increasing the stock of sheep.

From the *Inverness Courier* of 15th August 1850

> The rent of the (club) farm was £100 and the tenants were bound collectively for it. The amount of stock was limited in the aggregate but not individually. If the proper share of stock to each man was 100 and if No 1 had only 50 sheep on the hill, then No 2 might have 150. Some of the tenants may have been more fortunate in their stock than others or more provident in their management. But if their neighbours circumstances declined then the other tenants liability increased.....Club tenants if they had the unanimity of purpose, have seldom the means to stock their possessions with superior breeds of stock kept by their wealthier rivals in the trade; whilst from the system they follow, each man treating his own little flock as he pleased and selling when he chose, the stock never could attain that character without which good remunerating prices cannot be got.

From 1790 to 1815 there was a boom period in the Highlands with strong demand for sheep and wool, leading to sheep farmers competing for land at high rents and a trend towards longer leases. Cattle prices were high, illicit whisky had a good market and men were needed to serve in the overseas conflicts. But most of this Highland boom was due to ephemeral wartime conditions and much of the region's export economy fell apart with the coming of peace. Cattle prices halved between 1810 and 1830, legislation in 1823 restricted the manufacture of illicit whisky and the demobilisation of a vast number of servicemen put pressure on food resources. In addition kelp (seaweed), the great staple export of the Hebrides which had been the mainstay of Seaforth's Lewis

6 NAS RD2-293-00164

property, met with stiff opposition from imports. The demand for wool however was maintained, but in Strathconon sheep farming seems to have gone through a bleak period.

Strathconon was said to be one of the most congested areas of the Highlands (Mackenzie, 1883) and the population remained high throughout the early part of the 1800s; in 1829 it was reported to be 1100[7]. Eighty five births were recorded in the Old Parish Records for the upper part of the glen in the ten years between 1820 and 1830.

Many landowners supported education of the tenantry on their estates; they saw it as a means to improving the lot of their people by encouraging literacy and introducing new ideas. But often education was met by a dogged determination on behalf of the tenantry to stay with old habits and customs. On the Gairloch estate Dr John Mackenzie observed

> some parents were reluctant to send their children to school for fear of losing them as soon as they became educated enough to take off into the outside world…..some of them say they require the children to stay at home to help them in tilling the ground and the smaller ones to take care of their younger brothers and sisters. And after that….the taking home of the peats (Byam Shaw, 1988, p288).

In 1824 Patrick Butter visited the school in Strathconon. He was commissioned by the Scottish Society for the Propagation of Christian Knowledge (SSPCK) to inspect the Society's schools in the Highlands and Islands. The SSPCK was established in 1709 to spread the protestant religion - local heritors (landowners) supplied a school room and schoolmaster's house, while the SSPCK provided a teacher. Until 1767 teaching in Gaelic was forbidden but by 1760 the Society was printing and distributing the bible in Gaelic. By 1826 the Society had 134 schools. Butter's report for the school in Strathconon reads[8]

> The teacher was on vacation when I visited. The previous week 39 pupils had attended and 61 during the winter. The teacher who was 24 had two years service with the SSPCK. His house and school were small and in poor repair. The state of the roads and the travelling made it impossible for some children to come to school.

Butter noted that no one from over 80 families in the area could read. For this reason and due to widespread ignorance of the value of education the teacher did not impose school fees.

The documentary record for the 1820s is fragmentary but it seems to have been a time of hardship. By 1831 multiple tenancies in Strathconon had become a thing of the past and there seems to have been a more ruthless attitude towards the letting of tacks. Larger sheep farms were let and in creating these the landlord had reorganized the tenants so that they coexisted beside the sheep in congested communities, each one possessing a smaller piece of land. From 1834 to 1844 Colin Munro Esq was paying rent of £410 for Corriefeol, Achness and Scardroy in the upper glen and also Inverchoran and Carnoch[9]. In 1892 Duncan Campbell gives evidence to the Deer Commission

> Colin Munro put the tenants away from Coire Feola, Achad an Eas and Scaird Ruadh before 1839 (Royal Commission, 1892)

[7] Evidence of James Smith to the Royal Commission, 1892
[8] Patrick Butter's Journal: Strathconnan School report, 5 June 1824, available on Scran website www.scran.ac.uk
[9] NAS GD433-1-108 Strathconon Rental 1839

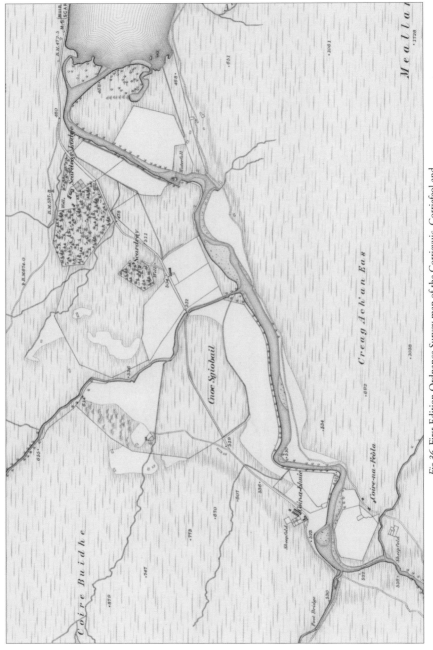

*Fig 36.* First Edition Ordnance Survey map of the Corrievuic, Corriefeol and Scardroy area in the upper glen – surveyed 1875 printed 1881

In the census of 1841 there were two households with nine people at Corriefeol, but at nearby Corrievuic (Corriebhuic) there were 14 households and 64 people; almost certainly they were evicted people who had congregated at Corrievuic. James Smith, factor for the Strathconon estate, in his evidence to the Deer Commission stated

By 1842 the congestion and poorness of the people, and there being no prospect of its being otherwise relieved, caused a number of small tenants who occupied the farm of Corriewick (Corrievuic) extending to 5500 acres to voluntarily give it up (Royal Commission, 1892)

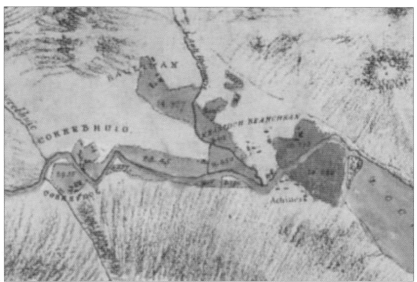

*Fig 37.* Extract from a "Plan of the estate of Strathconan" by Flint 1825, NAS RHP 2525, showing Scardoy and Corrievuic/Corriefeol area in upper Strathconon. Reproduced by kind permission of AM Brander

By 1851 the population of Corrievuic had been reduced to seven households and 19 people. James Smith commented that there were no evictions, the people had probably just drifted away.

Lower down the glen the tack of Invermeinie (Inverveinie), which included Glen Meinich, and Balblair was let in 1833 to John Fraser Esq. paying a rent of £130[10] and shortly after there was a significant reduction in the population of this part of the glen. As with Corrievuic, overcrowding was to develop in nearby townships, the 1841 census has 54 people at Blar-na-Beithe and 37 at Inverchoran. Finlay Mackay, a crofter at Drynie Park, Mulbuie on the Black Isle stated in his evidence to the Napier Commission (1884).

this place (Drynie Park) was first colonised about the year 1834 when a general clearance in Strathconon under gross circumstances sent the people adrift and a number of them, my late father among them, settled here. 21 families were cleared from Glencarnie (this name is not known in Strathconon, but it does seem

[10] NAS GD46-1-343 and GD433-1-108

to bear some resemblance to a combination of Invervannie/Glenveinie and Carnoch!).

Many of the people turned out of Strathconon in these years were to settle on the Mulbuie Common on the Black Isle, each being given from six to 18 acres of wasteland at a low rent. They set about establishing smallholdings by reclaiming what was originally a combination of trees and bleak heathery moorland. Some Strathconon people almost certainly emigrated to Canada at this time; Pictou, in Nova Scotia, was settled mainly by people from Ross-shire in the early 1830s[11]. No specific mention of people from Strathconon was found in the passenger lists of the ships but almost certainly they would have been amongst those emigrating. In 1848 more people were to leave for Australia; *The Witness* of 14 June 1848 reports that "People from Lochaber, Strathglass and Strathconon are leaving for Australia".

The reduction in the population of Strathconon in the first part of the 19th century seems to have passed relatively unrecorded. Landlords usually gave short term leases and could simply terminate a tenancy when the lease came up for renewal or a family could be evicted if their rents fell into arrears. The majority of the reduction seems to have been achieved by attrition - the people just drifted away. James Smith in his evidence to the Royal Commission (1892) reports that "the population was reduced in 1834 to 870 and by 1839 to 568". This was still a large population to be supported in addition to sheep.

*Fig 38.* Storage pits at Achness, thought to be for potatoes

The 1841 census records 220 people living in the upper glen where today there are perhaps ten. How did they survive? Almost certainly they would have relied heavily on the potato. Potatoes were introduced to Scotland in about 1750. They had the

[11] In June 1830 the Inverness Journal reported that 621people had left for Canada from Cromarty and between 1831 and 1835 no less than 14 ships arrived in Pictou laden with emigrants who had left the Highlands from Cromarty.

advantage over the usual crop of oats in giving a bigger yield per acreage of ground and would therefore feed three times the number of people. They were also well suited to the damp climate of the Highlands and readily cultivated on any type of soil. The potato was ideally suited to Strathconon where cultivatable land was at a premium. Eighty three storage pits were recorded at six different settlements in the upper part of Strathconon; they vary in size from 1m to 2m diameter and from 0.5m to 0.8m deep and are always situated in airy positions on the edge of well drained terraces or moraines. Similar pits occur throughout Highland glens, particularly in the Northeast. Very little research has been carried out on this type of site, and although it has not been proved, the pits are confidently assumed to be for storing potatoes. Achness has 22 pits, Invermeinie 17, Blarnabee 12, Corrievuic 8 and East Carnoch 8 pits. These are all settlements that experienced dense population numbers in the early part of the 19th century. The population would have relied heavily on the crop and almost certainly stored it for the winter months.

The illicit distillation of whisky was a further means by which the people survived. Our discovery of at least 48 illicit still sites provided evidence that the practice played a big part in the economy of the glen. More details of these and the history of distillation in Strathconon are covered in Chapter 10. Illicit distilling was a clandestine operation and there is very little in the documentary record, but we can get some understanding of the individuals involved from the number of cases brought to court for "the crime of assaulting, beating, wounding, obstructing and deforcing the Officers of the Revenue". The following were noted from the High Court and North Circuit minute book[12]

> September 1818 – John and Duncan Finlayson of Inverveinie, Donald MacLennan of Balblair, Duncan Macdonald of Inverchoran, also Donald Macdonald of Inverchoran, and Murdoch and Donald Macdonald of Milntown of Strathconnon
>
> April 1819 – Kenneth MacIvor of Inverveinie.
>
> September 1825 – Roderick Mackay – Crannich (transported for 7 years), John MacIver of Inverveinie, Kenneth Beaton of Balblair and Donald Beg Mackay of Dalnacroich (transported for 7 years)
>
> October 1831 – Donald Mackay of Invermeinie, Alexander Mackay of Balblair, Finlay MacIver and Alexander Campbell (or MacIver) of Invermeinie and Donald Mackay of Crannich

Temporary migration was certainly another of the mainstays of survival for the people of the glen at this time. Military recruitment continued but to a much lesser extent than in previous years and, in the main, income came from other forms of employment. From many writings it is clear that seasonal migration in search of work was a significant factor for many in the Highlands. Tom Devine (1988, p156) notes

> Great numbers of young men migrated to find work in the fishing industry of Caithness and the East coast. Many went south and east for agricultural labour or for short periods in the autumn to help with the harvest.

Highland girls were sought after as domestic servants in urban households. As the century progressed other opportunities arose in the developing industrial areas of the south.

[12] NAS JC 11-59-6 and JC 11-59-12

References to temporary migration from Strathconon are made by Devine (1988)

> The inhabitants of the parish of Carnoch…..contrive to subsist in summer by going in search of work to Edinburgh, Glasgow, Paisley, to railways, harvest work, by driving cattle to the south country markets or by fishing in Caithness.

And Richards and Clough (1989, p226)

> They (the people of Strathconon) were reported as having accumulated considerable reserves of money in the bank "made by labour on the railways in the south".

The coming of the railways provided employment opportunities

> For men, navvying on the railways had assumed great significance by the early 1840s and was to become even more important during the construction "mania" of 1846-47. Railway work had two particular attractions. First it paid better than agricultural employment; in 1845 weekly earnings in railway construction in the SE region averaged 30% more than harvest rates in the same area. Second and perhaps more crucially, the period of employment on the railway lasted longer. Even during the winter months operations continued except in the most inclement weather conditions. Thus during disturbances between Highland and Irish labourers in the Linlithgow area the legal authorities counted around 800 men from the Highlands in the district. At Cockburnspath on the Edinburgh to Berwick line, Irish strikers in 1845 were replaced by 300 Highlanders. More than half the 2100 men employed in railway construction in the Lothians were from the Highlands and in the same period they were also strongly represented among the navvy gangs on the Hawick branch of the North British and on the Caledonian lines (Devine, 1994, p143).

In December 1846 the *Inverness Courier* carried an advertisement "The Aberdeen Railway requiring 2,000 – 3,000 labourers".

But still the people in Strathconon were finding it difficult and becoming more destitute as the years progressed. Throughout this time many families were moving in with relatives and making no contribution to the rent of the croft. Conditions were becoming appalling and the *Inverness Courier* on 15th August , 1850 comments

> If the croft originally obtained by the head of the family was sufficient for the support of the family when the children were young, it is evident that if the children when they grew up and married, settled down one in the barn and another in the byre, displacing the cattle, the croft originally intended for one must be insufficient for three or more families. The share of a hill farm held by a club tenant, must have declined if the sons and daughters each had their flocks on the same hill, diminishing the number of sheep or cattle the original tenant, the father, could keep as his own. This is the course which the people have almost invariably followed…….It is in this manner that estates have become over-populated and landlords and people alike impoverished. Where the system has gone on unchecked by the managers of the land, forced emigrations have ultimately become necessary…….I have been in many parts of the Highlands but I never saw more dilapidated bothies (at Blar-na-Beithe), filthy outside and abominable within. Fever and other domestic miseries are inseparably associated

with dirt and discomfort and on the day I visited Blarnabee, three out of the five or six houses there, had cases of typhus fever. Yet the site of the town was elevated and dry and an invigorating mountain breeze swept down the glen sweet with perfume of the heather. It was a spot where health might have been sought if it was to be found anywhere; yet there, in the smoke and filth and foetid smells drawn by the strong sunshine from the pools and rotting heaps, fever in one of its most dangerous forms held down young and old.

Then in 1846 the potato crop failed. It was a poverty stricken population that could ill afford further problems. The *Inverness Courier* for 15th August 1850

It is admitted that even had there been no potato failure the crisis could not have been long postponed.

The effects of this great subsistence crisis were to be felt in the Highlands over the next decade. During this period, as the United Kingdom was consolidating its position as the most advanced economy in the world, the inhabitants of the Highlands and Islands were reduced to serious destitution when blight destroyed the potato, their main source of food. The epic potato famine in Ireland the year before had caused thousands to die of starvation, but this was not to be the case in the Highlands as various relief agencies stepped in. In Strathconon, as with other glens, the people were even more reliant on the money brought in from employment in the south. Devine (1988, p156-157) writes

There is abundant evidence of a very substantial increase in temporary migration during the potato famine…..One of the significant features of the increase in temporary migration in 1846-47 was an alteration in age and social composition of the migrant group; traditionally most temporary migrants were young, single males and females and the majority of the heads of households who were involved seemed to be of the cottar class. More crofters trekked south and east in search of employment and heads of households participated to a much greater extent than before. Another feature was that the people stayed away from their Highland homes for longer as they went from one form of employment to another; work on railway construction for example merged into harvesting…….However by the end of 1847 the industrial recession was starting to take effect. In October of that year railway workers were being paid off and Highlanders were streaming home in large numbers. Railway construction virtually ceased by the end of 1847 and there was a sharp fall in the demand for seasonal workers in agriculture and fishing. By 1848 the country was plunged into deep industrial recession and the number of casual poor in Scotland relieved through the official Poor Law doubled between 1847 and 1848.

Gerald Balfour, the son of the Strathconon landowner, writes in 1892[13].

After the potato disease in 1846 the destitution on the estate was so great and the outlook so serious that my father determined to effect a complete reorganisation of the management of the estate.

This reorganisation involved the removal of 27 families, a total of 123 people, from the settlements of Blar-na-Beithe, Balnacraig, Milton, Porin, Dalnacroich, Glacour and Balnault. Gerald Balfour continues

[13] A written statement from Gerald Balfour appears in the evidence of Duncan Campbell to the Royal Commission, 1892

The essential condition of success was that the population should bear a reasonable relation to the capacity of the crofts together with the opportunities of earning wages from labour on the estate. In my father's judgement the number of inhabitants, reduced as it was, was still too large to fulfill this condition. He came to the conclusion that it must still be further diminished, and that the holdings of the small tenants must be rearranged, and the practice of squatting (ie allowing the children on marriage to settle upon the parent's holdings) must be abolished, 385 persons remained on the estate and that number has now dwindled to 233. All the old people were left on the estate, they have gradually died off. In consequence of my father's reforms in the management of the estate the people have been far more active minded (Royal Commission, 1892).

The removals of 1850 in Strathconon were one of the more high profile and controversial cases of clearance in the Highlands. A letter to the *Inverness Advertiser* 9th July, 1850 reads

Strathconan Clearances - It seems that there is still some work going on about the proprietor's Lodge; but not one of those (people) on whom the decree of ejection passed has been allowed to have work for a single day. It may be said, that the people of Strathconan had been supported for years by work supplied by him at great expense; but has he done anything except embanking the river – work which naturally falls on the proprietor not on the tenants; and in addition to this building lodges for his own accommodation and that of his friends, dressing out the grounds about the lodge at Dalbreck and the factor's house, and building residences for his menials and officials. To this day he has done nothing for the improvement of the holdings of the small tenantry. He has however been doing all he could to remove them from the class of independent small tenants to that of dependant labourers and cottars. He removed the tenants some years back from the farm of Inverchoran; and these either got shelter or land from their neighbours at Blarnabee or else were compelled to become dependent on their own labour for their support. He deprived the tenants on the farms of Miltown, Pourin and Dalnacroich of the best part of the hill ground enclosing their former pasture ground and converting it into a larch plantation. The next step was to deprive the tenants of Balncraig and Blarnabee of the whole of the hill ground leaving them only a small strip, partly arable, partly pasture, to support themselves and their families.

The *Inverness Courier* set down the circumstances of the reorganization in great detail on 15th August, 1850 under the heading "The State of Strathconon"

Four years ago (in 1846) the proprietor found it necessary to seriously consider the state of his property and the people upon it. The small tenants were getting into arrears and their effects had frequently to be sequestrated. The people were not accustomed to stated labour and did not manage their lands to advantage.... The landowner devised a plan which involved appointing a new factor (James Smith).... An inquiry extended to every family and person on the estate with a view of ascertaining who were able, conjointly, and by their own labour and that of their families to maintain themselves on crofts without hill-ground. Those who being old and helpless should remain on the estate as dependents and those who having means and strength and youth to provide for themselves, but for whom there was no room on their old lands might be removed without injury or injustices to themselves. The tenancy was not renewed of two farms, Dromanriach and Achlorachan, which were held by one tenant who was a man of means and a desirable tenant in every respect but that he was non-resident…..It was part of the plan that the tenants should be assisted to build new and improved houses; and that when the hills of Glacour and Balnault should be given over to the new tenants money should be lent to them as it has to the larger tenants for hill drainage and that new regulations should be enforced in the management of those farms by which their stock might be improved….This then was the spirit in which the recent proceedings were conceived and I am at a loss to conceive the blame attached to them.

The people were informed of the plan and over the next four years preparations were made. Part of the plan in these years was putting the able bodied men to work and instructing them in good practices….At a time when those notices were given not a man in the glen was accustomed to stated daily labour. They reasoned that they had not been so used when they were young and it was not without difficulty they were got to persevere. They were ignorant of the use of the implements. The works were trenching and draining land on the farm of Dalbreck[14], cutting new channels for streams and embanking the channel for the river. One or two strangers were at first employed to instruct the native people but the latter rapidly improved. The strangers were then sent away and one of themselves who proved apt and clever took charge of the workmen and still continues to do so. Every willing person was employed at the highest current wages; by this course three purposes were served – whilst the estate was improved, the people were carried safely over a trying time of destitution and those who would have been helpless if turned from the glen three years ago were taught to be able to earn their bread elsewhere by their own labour. Some of those who have been thus taught have been removed

The unpleasant task of removal took place on Lammas Day, 1st August 1850…..Some of those who had been made aware that they must remove prepared to do so, but others were naturally unwilling to leave the scenes amidst which they had grown up. The legal proceedings were procrastinated that the people who were not then prepared to remove might be induced to promise to go away quietly at a future day. So anxious was Mr Smith to induce the people to give promises to this effect rather than to eject them summarily and so successful in obtaining either written or verbal pledges that during three days only three houses were pulled down in the whole glen and only four families who refused to give a promise to remove at any definite time were ejected by the officer.

[14] The government encouraged landowners to apply for loans, made available under the Drainage Act, to provide employment for the distressed people of the Highlands. These loans were made at favourable rates of interest and were to be repaid over 22 years.

On Lammas Day the *Inverness Courier* dispatched their reporter to the glen to witness the proceedings of removals. The newspaper had "from previous experience the utmost confidence of his (the reporter's) impartiality and discrimination" and he was afforded every facility in his inquiries. The original lessees of Blarnabee numbered five, there were three sub-tenants and four families who had "squatted down" beside them without land and paying no rent - 58 persons in total. The reporter in his article for the *Inverness Courier* 15th August 1850, gave a graphic and detailed account of the removal of six of the families and finished by saying

> Thus terminated the proceedings conducted throughout, I am bound to say, in a creditably humane spirit – every desire being shown, whilst carrying out the plans long before fixed upon, to do so in the least objectionable way……..From all the other parts of the property the total number of families removed was 21 – namely four tenants and 17 sub-tenants and cottars. Two of these sub-tenants and two of the cottars were from the farm of Dalbreck. One cottar from Balnacraig received a croft at Pourin and three remained as labourers. The 17 others removed were from the farms of Milton, Pourin and Dalnacroich and from Glacour and Balnault.

Mr Balfour and Mr Smith's desire is that the larger farms are held by resident tenants. They wish to encourage industrious habits and have made Glacour and Balnault no longer one but two farms to be held by club-tenants. The arable ground of Milton, Pourin and Dalnacroich is divided among 19 tenants making the population of these three towns 95 in all. To the old arable ground 17 acres of new land, all that is available, is to be added. The miller, the blacksmith and the schoolmaster are to have the smaller of the crofts of about three acres each, the other crofts average from six to seven acres each. At Glacour and Balnault the tenants are required to build new houses for themselves – the proprietor giving £10 to each tenant to aid him in doing so, and stones are at his command. These houses are built in better situations and are to be much larger and more comfortable than the old, bearing more resemblance to English cottages than Highland huts…... The club-tenants will receive money for hill-drainage on the same terms as the larger tenants. The stock managed by a shepherd will be gathered clipped smeared, marked and wintered as one stock and when sold the profits equally divided. In this way managed, the sheep and wool will be of uniform quality and both will acquire a character in the market. Whilst attentive to these matters, the proprietor has not neglected the educational interests of the young, an excellent schoolroom has been erected in the middle of the three towns and a young man appointed as teacher.

I think Mr Balfour has acted wisely and with much liberality – that the late proceedings will increase the comfort and future happiness and prosperity of the estate – and that in the performance of the disagreeable duty which fell to him Mr Smith has acted with prudence and leniency and with much consideration for the natural affections……In August 1849 the number of families on the estate was 116 and the entire population was 506. As has already been stated 27 families or

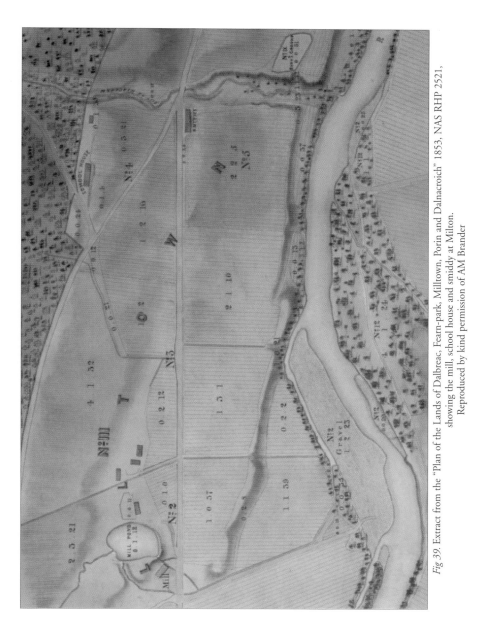

*Fig 39.* Extract from the "Plan of the Lands of Dalbreac, Fearn-park, Milltown, Porin and Dalnacroich" 1853, NAS RHP 2521, showing the mill, school house and smiddy at Milton. Reproduced by kind permission of AM Brander

in all 123 persons including children have been removed, thus leaving 385 persons on the property. This may be a "clearance" but I am more inclined to regard it as a restoration of the glen to a sound condition or at least a decided step towards that objective.

In 1851 the population in the glen had been reduced to 385, a third of what it had been 50 years previously. The twenty-four families who left Strathconon found refuge at Knockfarrel, near Loch Ussie, where they were provided with holdings on marginal land by Lady Stafford of the Cromartie Estate. The family of Finlay MacIver was one of them; his story is told in Chapter 13. By all accounts all the families did very well as, thirty years later, William Gunn, factor of the Cromartie Estate, in his evidence to the Napier Commission (1884) observed

they have proved to be excellent tenants in every respect. They are industrious and farm systematically and well and of this we have the best evidence in the fact that they pay their rents regularly and that within the last few years most of them have substantially improved their houses, four of which have lately been slated

The photograph of the houses at Balnault in about 1880, together with the 1st edition OS map, give a good impression of one of the settlements after the "modernizations" of the 1850s. Six families were settled at Balnault and required to build themselves "modern" houses which "bear more resemblance to English houses". A further photograph (Fig. 32) of a cottage at Strathanmore c1870-1880 exists and is a good example of the old Scottish type of stone house. This cottage has disappeared completely and been replaced by a flood prevention bank containing the Allt an t-Strathain Mhor.

*Fig 40.* Extract from the first Edition OS survey, 1881, showing the buildings at Drumanriach and Balnault, now destroyed to make way for Loch Meig

*Fig 41.* Photograph, c.1880, of Balnault

# 10. "Still-Life" in Strathconon
## – the story of illicit whisky production

Within a small wooded glen in lower Strathconon there is a landscape which appears to have been devoted to the production of illicit whisky. An area of roughly half a square kilometre has four probable still sites, ten small farmsteads, two kilns and a possible industrial site of unknown purpose. In the wider area of 2 square kilometres a further eight probable still bothies have been identified. All the remains are in a wasted state and in the summertime most are covered with bracken or heather. But in this landscape it is possible to get a glimpse of the life that the illicit distillers or "smugglers", used to live, as they carried out their clandestine activity of 200 years ago. Strathconon was well known for being a hotbed of "smuggling", it is said to have been a "no-go" area for the excise man and the people would have been free to go about their illicit business without disturbance. Our discovery of nearly 50 still sites in the glen was just one of the many highlights of the project. In addition an elderly resident of the glen remembered her grandfather showing her a small glen where the smugglers had carried out their illicit business, bringing home the fact that the practice had been taking place in the not too distant past!

*Fig 42.* A sketch of an illicit still by Sir Edwin Landseer, 1827

First a brief description of the processes involved in distilling whisky is needed. The ingredients required are grain, usually barley (or its variation, bere), a constant supply of running water and a plentiful supply of peat. The barley is allowed to germinate into malt which is then dried by gently heating it. The dried malt is milled to make "grist", and this is then mixed with hot water to make "wort". The "wort" is fermented and the resulting "wash" is heated up in a still, preferably made of copper, although many of the illicit variety were made of tin. The alcohol vapours are cooled by passing them through a "worm" which has cold water running over it and the spirit is collected from a spout at the bottom of the "worm".

The archaeological remains of still bothies are often difficult to identify. Many of the stills would have been improvised affairs with no regular form and the apparatus of pot-still and worm will have been removed. The only consistent features of the sites are that they are in secret, remote locations and close to a source of running water. Most of the sites in Strathconon are rectangular buildings of rough dry stone or turf construction, usually about 7m x 5m in size. Generally they are recessed into a bank or slope or against a crag, so that they could have been easily camouflaged by covering them with branches and turves.

The still bothies in the lower glen are found in wooded areas and although the terrain is rough they are easily accessible. In one particular area, the small steep glen mentioned above, there is evidence of more permanent settlement with several small farmsteads. Many of these have an associated enclosure and a small patch of improved ground close by. The process of distilling took place most commonly in late autumn when the harvest was gathered in and when the burns were in spate; during the rest of the year the people would have worked a farmstead on a small scale, growing a crop or two and perhaps keeping a cow. Also in this small glen we were surprised to find a substantial kiln with a complex arrangement of barns attached to it. There is very little cultivatable land and no indication of limestone in the vicinity; could it be that this kiln was associated with the distilling process?

The still bothies in the upper glen tend to be bigger than those in the lower glen and are located in more remote mountain terrain. Strathconon is a U-shaped valley and the sites are very often just above the lip of the U, tucked away in a bend of a burn, possibly so that the smoke could not be seen from below. Many of the bothies have a curved recess in one of the rear corners and some have a raised platform in the recess. In one particular bothy there is a stone lined oval recess 1.5m x 1m x 0.5m deep which almost certainly would have contained some sort of vessel. Also in this same bothy there is a shallow stone lined fire pit – other bothies may have similar fire pits but it is difficult to be certain from the surface features. Only at one bothy is there a definite stone lined lade to deliver running water to the site, otherwise very little evidence of lades was detected, they may have been of iron or wood which has long since perished.

*Fig 43.* The remains of a probable illicit still bothy above Balnault

*Fig 44.* A stone lined lade supplying water to an illicit still bothy in the lower glen

*Fig 45.* The remains of a probable illicit still bothy in the lower glen

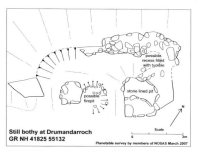

*Fig 46.* Plan of an illicit still bothy in the lower glen.

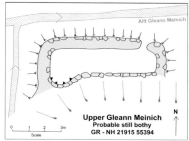

*Fig 47.* Plan of an illicit still bothy in the upper reaches of Gleann Meinich showing the curved recess in the rear corner.

*Fig 48.* The remains of a probable illicit still bothy above Milton

Osgood Mackenzie (1921) recalls

> in Ross-shire a distillery had regularly built low stone walls, water-tight heather thatch, iron pipes leading cold spring water to the still rooms and such an array of casks, tubs etc as told that gaugers never troubled their owners.

Some of the bothies had significant tumble internally suggesting deliberate destruction and at a few of the sites, particularly those in remote locations, there were the remains of a second bothy; these may have been living quarters or sleeping accommodation. At other sites there were associated structures which could have been stores, hiding places or "look-outs".

The tradition of distilling whisky on a small scale for family and local consumption goes back several centuries in the Highlands. In 1780 the government made small stills illegal and increased the tax on the malt used for distilling. The quality of the legal whisky became inferior but yet it was more costly. Throughout the Highlands, rising population, fewer employment opportunities and substantial increases in rent compelled a search for alternative sources of income. The increasing demand for Highland whisky provided that alternative. The production of whisky went underground and illicit distillation flourished from 1780 to 1823. The fact that illicit distillation was a clandestine activity was all to the good because earnings from it were less readily estimated by avaricious landlords who would increase the rents. Some argue that the element of risk involved in illegal practices lent a certain colour to drab lives

> It presents all the fascination of the gaming table….. In smuggling there is a spirit of adventure and hazard which has the charm for the mind of the peasantry. An escape or a successful resistance is remembered as heroic achievement; men encourage each other and a fraternity of feeling is produced among them by a sense of common danger (Stewart of Garth, 1829, p360)

Often the whole family was involved with the womenfolk playing a big part in producing the spirit and the children keeping a look-out for intruders or "gaugers", as the government excise men were known. Numerous stories are recounted of the adventures of the illicit distillers in the execution of their trade; fake funeral processions travelled long distances with the spirit concealed in the coffin and women were seen going to market with sudden advanced "pregnancies".

Farquhar MacLennan, also known as the Ross-shire Wanderer or Fearchair A Ghuna, a distinctive character who roamed the roads of the Black Isle and the Beauly Firth in the early part of the 19th century, was involved in distilling whisky and was to experience several encounters with excise officers from which he seems to have come off relatively lightly. He was born in Strathconon in 1784 to a family of smugglers and spent his first 25 years in the glen. He received little by way of education, apart from the more practical subjects of shooting, distilling whisky and agriculture. He became well known for his witty, sarcastic comments and on one occasion he was interviewed by Excise men in Dingwall about the burning of a cottage near his home in Strathconon. Threatened with "decapitation" he retorted "you will get all the information from my head that you can but you will get none from me". His father however, betrayed by a neighbour, was heavily fined for smuggling and had his implements and produce confiscated (Anon, 1881).

By its very nature illicit distilling was secretive and no records were kept, but we are fortunate in having the contemporary observations of two influential people who had close experience of the situation in Ross-shire, Sir George Mackenzie of Coul, near Contin, and Hugh Munro of Teaninich, near Alness. Both gave evidence to the Parliamentary Enquiry of 1822[1]. Sir George Mackenzie was unwell at the time and gave written evidence; he had "thirty years residence among smugglers or illicit distillers in Ross-shire and was acquainted with the subject minutely". Hugh Munro attended Edinburgh in person to give his evidence under oath; he "had resided in Ross-shire ever since 1795 and been connected with the distillery at Teaninich since Nov 1817", almost certainly he would have had a vested interest in painting a "black picture". Sir George writes

> The entire home consumption of spirits in the County of Ross continues to be supplied by illicit distillation.

Hugh Munro was aware that

> There is not a justice of the peace who can say that he does not in his own family consume illegally made spirits.....illicit distillation is going on to a very great extent in this part of the country and I think it is increasing......they (the illicit distillers) are generally composed of small highland farmers, persons to whom these farmers give a but to live in, and many desperate characters. Strathconan and Strathglass are both great smuggling districts.....They probably do not distil on the farm but upon some concealed part of the highlands; in the highlands there are numberless recesses and inlets where they carry on their illicit distillation. In the hills of the neighbourhood of highland farms they build a hut which is common to the smugglers of that district; when one person finishes his smuggling or what he calls his broust, the next neighbour does the same; they take it in turns. They pass the night in watching the whisky pot and in drinking, a constant state of intoxication and carousing is kept up.........Every 8 to 10 days a supply of barley from the south goes up to Strathconan and Strathglass to the smugglers. The dealers bring vessels loaded with barley into the Beauly Firth; they then send scouts out to give notice of where the vessel is lying and the illicit distillers come down and buy it.

There was a similar clandestine network of distribution of the finished product. After distillation the product was conveyed to market by regularly trained smugglers, normally strangers from outside the district of manufacture and generally Irishmen or Lowlanders. Heavily armed convoys thirty to forty strong carried the liquor to Lowland towns.

Inevitably the illegal practice was to have an effect on the population. Sir George writes

> The children are taught to lie and steal and poach and kill fish from their infancy. They see their parents live in the constant breach of the laws and thus pay no regard to the laws themselves.......The morals of the peoples of the Highlands have undergone a great change since the prevalence of illicit distillation; it is clear

[1] British Parliamentary Papers Vol VII "Inquiry into the Revenue Arising in Ireland etc", 1823.

to all who are acquainted with them. Formerly they were mild sober and inoffensive: now they are daring profligate and full of insubordination; insomuch that in same parts a sheriff's officer dare not execute summons of removing and an informer was even lately murdered.....These parts are accordingly nests of vice. The farms are reduced by sub sets to mere patches the occupiers of which live by smuggling........It was reported that, in Strathconan, 15 bottles a day are distilled by smugglers, amounting to 120 ankers of nine gallons each week. The whisky is openly carried to market by smugglers escorted by armed men in defiance of the laws...... When going about here I often meet smugglers returning with their empty casks, they go down during the night but return openly during the day.

In Hugh Munro's opinion

It is not possible to conceive a school of rebellion greater or worse than the smuggling.

Landowners encouraged Illicit distillation in both highland and lowland areas. In the highland smuggling areas they "turning a blind eye" to the practice as it provided cash for the tenant to pay an inflated rent and in the nearby fertile areas of Easter Ross and the Black Isle it provided a market for barley at an inflated price. Sir George again

Even the sheriff of the county, Mr MacLeod of Geanies, encourages it; his carts have been seen carrying his grain upwards of 20 miles to be disposed of to the smugglers and when remonstrated with on the subject he answered "How then do you suppose we sell our barley?" This gentleman has for more than 50 years been in receipt of £400 a year from the Government for carrying the laws into effect.......Both the low country and the highland proprietors accordingly attend the excise courts not for the purpose of carrying the laws against illicit distillation into effect but to protect their own interests by an evasion of the laws. Accordingly the excise provincial courts have long become an absolute farce. Fines were imposed merely to save appearances and not with any hope that they would suppress the evil in question.

The dilemma of the justices at Dingwall was put by Sir George in his evidence

Having daily opportunities of observing its ruinous effects, our anxiety to suppress illicit distillation is very great, but when we sit in judgement and we see before us our own tenants, we know that when we inflict even the lowest penalty, if the tenant is able to pay then he is not able to pay his rent and if he is not able to pay we must send him to prison where he can do nothing to help his affairs; in the meantime his family is starving on account of being deprived of help or attempting to find relief by conduct far worse than defrauding the revenue. In punishing delinquents under the laws of excise we are directly bringing ruin on our tenantry; if our tenants fall we must fall along with them.

The excise man, given their difficult task in such circumstances, had abandoned trying to enforce the law and many had resorted to exploiting the situation themselves. Sir George observed

The Act of Parliament leaves it in the discretion of the officer to destroy the utensils if he thinks proper. It is commonly observed in our country that the utensils are not destroyed; were they to be destroyed it would throw many obstacles in the way of the illegal distiller and in, many instances prevent him going on with his work….. Every utensil of every description should be destroyed and nothing allowed to be carried away as a prize……It was an easy matter for an officer to appropriate for himself a great part of the malt duties with very little risk of detection for how could each sum he receives at different periods from perhaps 500 small smugglers be proved…..It is said that in Ross-shire, the smugglers wives sent presents of veal, poultry, whisky, butter and cheese to the wives of the officers in return for information about a visit from the excise……the illicit trade has now reached a length in many parts of the Highlands particularly in Strathconan, that it is dangerous for an excise officer to make a seizure or to attempt to demolish the utensils.

And Hugh Munro says

In several straths such as Strathconan, Strathcarron and etc, the excise officers are now often deforced and dare not attempt to do their duty as the smugglers are too strong; smuggled whisky is openly carried to market by smugglers escorted by armed men in defiance of the laws…..There was an officer at my distillery, who had been for a short time in Strathconan, he told me that no officer could do his duty in that quarter and last year I was informed by another officer that he was obliged to retire being confronted by a large party of smugglers who were escorting spirits with nearly 20 horses.

There was inadequate provision for the courts to operate effectively, fines and punishments were hardly ever imposed. Hugh Munro noted

I have seen acts of illicit distillation fined at no more than £1 to £3-5 and often if the smuggler had good interest at court he has got off without a fine at all…..The courts (in Dingwall) are not held very often; some years back I have seen a great number of cases, I think I may safely say, there were 100 in one day.

Sir George reports that

The excise officers, for what reason I cannot tell, allow cases to accumulate to a prodigious number before the justices are called upon; the consequences of this is hurry, confusion and a very imperfect justice……The accommodation for our prisoners, at from 50 to 100, is not at present sufficient in the counties and our jails are quite inadequate to contain the numbers who are sometimes convicted.

Sir George relates a story about a different approach that was tried in his neighbourhood

Because of the expense and trouble of hunting about the mountains for stills a different plan was tried two or three times with complete success; the distillers were allowed to carry on their processes without molestation and night patrols were established on the roads; this country is easily watched on account of the rivers forcing the people to pass at particular places; watches were set at all the passes into the low country and the finished article was seized.

But whilst being successful on some occasions, this action did not always produce the required result. Sir George also reports that those who were watching have seized the spirits and gone away with their booty instead of destroying it on the spot and seeking the smuggler……In every point of view the manner in which the excise department is conducted is a perfect farce, the smugglers are a privileged set allowed by the proprietors and gaugers almost to do as they like, all the efforts are directed to useless checks on the licensed distillers as if the fair traders and not the smugglers were the enemies of their country.

From 1818 there is also the evidence of several court cases relating to "the crime of assaulting, beating, wounding, obstructing and deforcing the Officers of the Revenue". These mention the individuals involved by name and their place of residence; occasionally the general area in which the offence took place will be named, but never the precise location.

In one court case a map which marks a "smugglers hut or bothie" has been located[2]. It is the only still bothy for which we have positive documentary evidence, but yet, on the ground, the bothy is the least convincing of the sites as it was almost totally constructed of turf and has a very amorphous form. The map was produced in connection with a murder case, which appears to have been a tragic accident involving two individuals making their way home on a winter's night in December 1834 after imbibing their produce! Their journey is marked on the map, with annotated details of events, and a comprehensive account of the trial of Duncan Grant of Achlorachan appeared in the *Inverness Journal* on April 24, 1835. He was accused of the murder of James Macdonald, also of Achlorachan, and brought to trial in Dingwall Sheriff Court in March 1835. Grant and Macdonald had been at work in the hills above the township together with at least four others; the smugglers' bothy was remotely located at Loch Chor-lea, 3 kilometres north of Achlorachan. Both had partaken of the finished whisky and had left the hut sometime after 3am in an intoxicated state to proceed home. Somewhere between the hut and the ruins of a bothy called Blatach, James Macdonald had collapsed and Grant took him on his back and carried him until he himself became so fatigued and overcome with the liquor that he could no longer continue. Macdonald was laid inside the ruined hut at Blatach, covered with dry moss and turf to keep him warm and Grant then went to Macdonald's house to inform his parents. Angus Macdonald, father of the deceased, recollected that the prisoner had called at his house about Christmas, a little before daylight and told him that he had left their son at Blatach. He and his wife went up to Blatach, but concluded that their son was dead; they noted signs of a struggle and a red mark around his neck. Mr.McDougall, on behalf of the prisoner, contended that the deceased was intoxicated and that Grant had assisted him (the deceased), and being himself intoxicated, his assistance might not have been rendered in the most judicious manner, he had hauled him along, carelessly and brutally. Nevertheless the prisoner was found guilty of culpable homicide and sentenced to four months' imprisonment.

New legislation in 1823 reduced the excise duty on malt and increased the powers of the courts. The powers of the excise man were also increased and he was encouraged to

[2] NAS RHP 140009

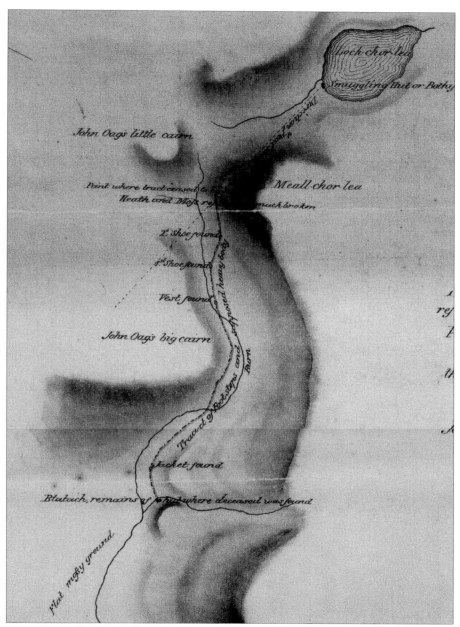

Loch chor-lea

Smuggling Hut or Bothy

John Oag's little cairn

Meall-chor lea

Point where tract ceased
Heath and Moss much broken

2ᵈ Shoe found

1ˢᵗ Shoe found

Vest found

John Oag's big cairn

Tract of foot-steps and supposed heavy body

Burn

Jacket found

Blatach, remains of a hut where deceased was found

Flat mossy ground

*Fig 49.* Extract from the sketch produced for the 1834 "murder" case, showing the route taken by the two men and the smuggling bothy at Loch Chor-lea (Loch a' Choire Leith). NAS RHP 140009

intervene more aggressively by using army and navy personel. In Ross and Cromarty specialised squads of sailors from the revenue cutter Atlanta helped to suppress the smuggling and the aid of the military from Fort George could be called upon. The decade after 1823 saw a series of violent incidents between the revenue service and groups of illicit distillers determined to tolerate no outside interference in their activities. The *Inverness Journal* reports an incident on 22nd May, 1829

> An Excise Officer and his party were deforced in Strathconon by the country people, who used so much violence as to render it necessary for the Excise party to leave without completing their survey, or destroying two illicit stills which they had discovered. On Friday the party again proceeded to the spot, but were met by a mob, chiefly of women, who poured showers of stones on them. The commander of the party, very properly retreated, finding it impossible to effect his object; he then sent off a messenger to Fort George, requesting that a party of the Royals, at present stationed there, should be sent to his assistance; accordingly, twenty-one rank and file marched to Strathconon, the stills were destroyed and a considerable quantity of spirits seized.

And a further incident on April 1st, 1831;

> An Excise Officer, assisted by two of the seamen belonging to the Revenue cutter, while on a survey in Strathconon, discovered a still at work; but on endeavouring to seize the spirits and destroy the utensils, the party was deforced, and obliged to retreat. Having however, been reinforced by two additional assistants, they revisited the bothy, where they found eight sturdy Highlanders round the fire – a scuffle ensued, and both parties were severely hurt, some of them to the danger of life. Two of the smugglers have been taken, and will probably be tried before the ensuing Circuit Court.

The practice of illicit distilling in Strathconon gradually died out and by 1837 the New Statistical Account for the Parish of Contin states

> For many years smuggling prevailed in the interior of the parish to an alarming extent and must have been hurtful to the morals of the people, but it has been so completely suppressed that illicit whisky has now become almost as rare as foreign spirits (Downie, 1837).

The new policy would appear to have been extremely successful. In general large scale whisky-making outside the law was doomed and there was a substantial expansion in the number of licensed malt whisky plants, no doubt encouraged by the absorption within the legal sector of the skills of the "sma still" operators of the illicit days. At the beginning of the 19th century illicit distilling was one of the means by which the large population of Strathconon was able to support itself; it probably made a contribution to delaying their inevitable departure from the glen.

# 11. The ecclesiastical background of Strathconon

Most of Strathconon is in the Parish of Contin but the ecclesiastical divisions in the past have been complex, and from early times the populated part of Dalbreac, Millton, Porin, Dalnachroich and Strathanmore was in Fodderty Parish with a small part, around Inverchoran and Invermeinie/Glenmeinie, in the quaod sacra Parish of Carnoch, which belonged to Urray Parish.

Contin Parish is one of the largest parishes in Ross-shire. The parish church at Contin is medieval in date and is likely to have been in existence when the parochial system was established in the Diocese of Ross in the 12th century. The church is dedicated to St Maelrubha who brought Christianity to the north of Scotland, founding a monastery at Applecross in AD 673.

Place names including the element Annat suggest that the earliest Christian presence in the area was further west in Strathconon; this place name is generally accepted to be a 9-10th century term for a church site. An Annait is recorded (Watson, 1904) immediately west of Balnacraig at NH 291532, 600m south of Carnoch Church. There are no visible ruins at this site but it is noted that it is located immediately below the dun at Creag Ruadh, possibly a late Iron Age seat of power in the glen.

Lower down the glen, at NH 3403 5481 east of Bridgend and south of the River Meig, are Carn na h'Annaite, Allt na h'Annaite, Clach na h'Annaite and Cladh na h'Annaite, the last being a formal burial ground, which is still visible as a rectangular area enclosed by a low wall. Oral tradition has it that this was the last resting place for unbaptised children. The burial ground suggests the former presence of a place of worship,

*Fig 50.* The burial ground at Porin, formerly known as Cladh Meinn

although place names translating as "of the Annat" are considered to refer to church lands rather than buildings.

Another former burial ground, at Scardroy, is indicated by the place name Cnoc a Mhinister. It is likely that until the Reformation of 1560 the parish church of Contin was supported by smaller chapels at Scardroy and at an Annait (Balnacraig) which possibly represented the centres of population in the medieval period. These chapels would have fallen out of use with the Reformation but the burial grounds probably continued to be used until the Clearances. A third early burial ground at Porin, formerly known as Cladh Meinn, is still in use. From the documentary record, Colin Mackenzie, the first Earl of Seaforth (c1594-1633) apparently laid the foundations for a church in Strathconon of which the walls

> are still to be seen in Main in Strathconon, the walls being built above the height of a man above the foundation and he had in mind to endow it further had he lived longer (Mackenzie, 1879)

It is possible that this building was located in the burial ground at Porin (Cladh Meinn).

Although most of the lands of Strathconon lie in Contin Parish, there were parts that were served by the Parishes of Urray and Fodderty. It is unclear when the central portion of the glen, the lands of Main, became part of Fodderty Parish but MacCoinnich (2009) writes

> in the 17th Century, the records of the presbytery of Dingwall give us the impression of disputes and difficulties between the different parishes over provision of pastoral care, with ministers appearing extremely reluctant to serve in Strathconon. The moderator of the Dingwall Presbytery in a meeting of 1666, commented that all the ministers present were 'diligent in their preaching and catechising save that Strathconon alone was neglected.' The presbytery did record that they were mindful that it was difficult for ministers to serve at Strathconon, and they seem to have built a house for itinerant ministers visiting the area.

## Carnoch Church[1]

The Telford Church at Druimfearn, Strathconon, is one of only 16 Parliamentary churches in the Highlands to survive. Some have been entirely demolished, three stand as roofless ruins, some have been converted to private dwellings and only a few are relatively unaltered.

In 1819 the General Assembly of the Church of Scotland petitioned the Government for aid towards the construction of additional churches and manses in the remote parts of the Highlands where the number of people frequently exceeded the capacity of the local parish churches. The Church of Scotland was also afraid that in certain areas the Roman Catholic Church would maintain or increase its presence where regular non-Catholic services were not available. In 1823 the Government passed an act for building additional churches in the Highlands and Islands of Scotland. This gave a budget of £50,000 for the building of 40 churches and manses and local landowners were encouraged to provide the land for their construction. A total of 42 churches and 41 manses were built by the time the work had been completed in 1835. The design and

[1] Much of the text for this piece on Carnoch Church is taken from Catherine Dagg, "Carnoch Church, Strathconon – Archaeological Investigation and Recording"

*Fig 51.* The Telford church, known as Carnoch, at Druimfearn near Strathanmore, Carnoch itself is a further 5 kms up the glen

construction was entrusted to the engineer Thomas Telford; largely due to the experience he had gained in the successful construction of roads and bridges throughout the Highlands some years earlier.

There are four Parliamentary churches in Ross-shire. The church and manse in Strathconon are in good condition. The exterior of the church is virtually unchanged but most of the original internal features have been removed. The other three churches in Ross-shire range in condition from good (Ullapool), through moderate (Kinlochluichart), to poor (Poolewe).

At the beginning of the 19th century Strathconon was considered to be densely populated in comparison to other Highland glens. The presbytery of Dingwall suggested Strathconon to the Parliamentary Commissioners as a site for one of the new churches in 1825. The then heritor, a trustee named James Stuart of Dunearn, was approached and was agreeable but hesitated about giving the land, with the result that Strathconon was replaced by Poolewe on

*Fig 52.* The Telford manse next to the church

the list. In 1828 the application was renewed and accepted. The *Inverness Journal* in July 1829 reported that "the Commissioners have a surplus (of funding) over which they intend to apply in building a church and manse at Carnoch in Strathconon. This they represent as a specially remote and needy district. With the building in Carnoch the report says the work of the Commissioners may be deemed final and complete"

The site of the present church may not be that which was originally intended. Local tradition believes that the site originally chosen was 5 kilometres further up the glen, on a prominent grassy platform at the bend of the glen (Grid reference NH 2597 5082), opposite Inverchoran and near Carnoch Farm. The story goes that, when the cart carrying the building materials became bogged down at Druimfearn, it was decided to build the church where the material came to rest! This may be true but the Register of Sasines dated January 1830 has the following entry: "The Parliamentary Commissioners get convey (sic.) to a regular piece of ground with the Church thereon and piece of ground to the east with the minister's manse thereon, being parts of the farm called Drumfearn in Strathconon".

John Mackenzie, formerly the missionary to Strathconon, was appointed as the first minister at Carnoch and for a while "the people are warmly attached to the Established Church" (Downie 1837) but 6 years later, in 1843, the records of the Kirk Session for Carnoch state "the Rev John Mackenzie, Donald Mackay and John Cameron met for devotional exercises, and in common with the vast majority of the people of God throughout the land renounced their connection with the Established Church of Scotland". They left the church after what was perceived to be injustices at the hands of the landowners. It is not surprising that the Disruption, a revolt against, among other things, the right of the heritor to choose the minister, was wholeheartedly supported in Strathconon. Dr Cameron Lees, 1856 – 1859, later recorded "The retiring minister had made his Celtic and obedient congregation hold up their hands and swear in solemn oath never to re-enter the church. Henceforth it was left desolate" (MacLean, 1922)

Despite the almost complete lack of a congregation, a succession of ministers was appointed to Carnoch. For various reasons the first five appointments were very short lived. Dr James Cameron Lees recalled later "the church at Carnoch was built with an eye to economy. None of these churches had wooden flooring. The pews were fixed to earth and the passages were flagged with stone. When the congregation left them they fell into decay. The damp oozed through the walls and oozed up through the earthen floor, rotting the pews". When Cameron Lees arrived he memorably held a service (in Gaelic) for one "a shepherd who had walked miles over the snow". He records "the number attending the services varied with the weather, I think there would be about 30 attending in fine weather. In summer the number was increased when the sportsmen and their servants came in the shooting season". Cameron Lees recalls "I have seen six members of the House of Lords in the congregation" (MacLean, 1922)

Six years after Cameron Lees's departure the Rev John MacDougall was admitted to Carnoch. Although originally a zealous worker he appears to have succumbed to the isolation of Strathconon and "shut himself into the manse and lived a hermit life". The congregation drifted away and the church bell ceased to be rung. He stopped attending to funerals, celebrated no marriages in 26 years and had not administered baptism for 12 years by the time he was suspended for inefficiency in 1897. The manse had fallen into a deplorable condition and the church was filthy. The description given to the Dingwall Presbytery by Captain Combe included "the seats and floor are covered in bird droppings and quite uncared for". Many of the windows had been smashed. In 1899 Captain Combe was persuaded to spend the sum of £730 on repairs to the church and manse. The new minister, John MacLean, appears to have been a prime mover in generating physical improvements to the church. He had a stove and an organ installed, and by 1919 "there was a trim church, manse and garden" (Dagg, 2006)

Of the congregation which walked away from the Established church in 1843, the majority would have left the strath in the removals between 1840 and 1851. The remainder were for the most part settled around Milton and Pourin where they probably built a meeting house for Free Church services (on the estate plan of 1853[2] a chapel is marked on the site of the present Free Church). In 1875 Arthur Balfour paid for the building of a Free Church manse (East manse) and in 1892 Captain Combe had a new Gothic style Free Church built, the present church, on the site of the original meeting house.

In 1900 the United Free Church separated from the Free Church and began worshipping in Strathconon Hall which was built at this time. Relations between the Established and United Free churches had warmed by the time of the 1914-18 War; when the minister of Carnoch, John Sellar, took up duty as a military chaplain with the Lovat Scouts for the duration of the war and the United Free Church minister, Mr Bethune, was invited to undertake pulpit and pastoral visits. By 1926 the 2 congregations were expressing a feeling to reunite. This union was carried out in 1927, with a service being held each Sunday at noon in Carnoch church and in the evening in the Hall. The Telford Church was made redundant as a place of public worship in the year 2000 and the manse is now a holiday house.

[2] NAS RHP 2521

*Fig 53.* Dalbreac Lodge c.1880. Reproduced by kind permission of AM Brander

*Fig 54.* Extract from the "Plan of the Lands of Dalbreac, Fearn-park, Milltown, Porin and Dalnacroich" 1853, NAS RHP 2521, showing Dalbreac Lodge and its environs.
Reproduced by kind permission of AM Brander

# 12. New landlords and new Initiatives - from sporting estates to hydroelectricity

Throughout the Highlands there was a transfer of estates to new landlords during the first half of the 19th century. The old order of Highland elite had been much more vulnerable to financial embarrassment than their peers in other regions. Some had invited criticism for living beyond their means, for their indulgence and wasteful expenditure and for their careless mismanagement of estates. Much debt also came from unsuccessful investments in the infrastructure of the estates, building roads and bridges, enclosure and drainage for example, and in the provision of relief for destitute tenancies during bad seasons. Debt had been a fact of life amongst most Highland proprietors in the 17th and 18th centuries. Much of the debt in the 19th century was inherited and a considerable amount of income was tied up in servicing the interest charges. In addition each estate was burdened with an array of annuities, life rents and portions for family members. It was usual to make allowances to younger sons and daughters and these had become unavoidable charges on an estate. In the period from 1790 to 1812 money had flooded into the Highlands as a result of spectacular increases in cattle prices, windfall gains from kelping, income from sheep farming, fishing and illicit distillation. Proprietors were able to demand higher rents from their tenants. But then just as dramatically the prosperity ebbed away in the 1820s. The hereditary elite of the society was financially doomed. The great land sales of this period were one result of this economic crisis.

From 1820 the pace of change in the pattern of landownership of Highland estates increased and over the next 40 years two-thirds of estates were to acquire new proprietors. Many families who had held extensive tracts of land for many generations disappeared from the scene and even those who managed to survive were forced into massive sales of parts of their heritage to maintain solvency. The pattern of landownership changed dramatically. Almost three-quarters of the area were now owned by a new breed of proprietor from outside the region. They were merchants, financiers, lawyers and industrialists from the Lowlands or from England, many of whom had made their fortunes in lucrative business overseas. They lavished expenditure on their estates and in the process helped to subsidise the local economy from the profits of trade in distant parts of the world.

The great transfer of Highland property was not simply due to an increase in number of estates on the market. Many of the affluent classes of Victorian Britain saw a Highland property as an investment and the value of a property was to increase with the massive growth of sheep farming and the expansion of deer forests. But for many the most significant reason for purchasing a Highland estate seems to have been that it was fashionable to view the Highlands with a romantic eye. The new interest in nature, appreciation of the picturesque landscape, the wilderness of scenic beauty with its romantic, historical and legendary associations led to the Highlands becoming an area where it was possible to commune with nature and achieve spiritual renewal. For the fashionable the attractions of the Grand Tour on the Continent were replaced by a visit to the mountains and rivers of the Highlands.

The region became a major centre for the physical sports of hunting, shooting and fishing – 28 deer forests were formed by 1839 and a further 16 in 1840 (Devine, 2006). It was said that "as soon as a man has amassed a fortune his first desire seems to be to buy or rent a deer forest in Scotland and there to gather his friends to enjoy his hospitality and sport". The Highlands possessed the qualities of remoteness and isolation but new transport facilities guaranteed reasonably quick connections from the great urban centres of the south. Coach services had improved significantly, by 1836 it was said that "a person might dine in Edinburgh one day and breakfast in Inverness the next" and the invention of the ocean going paddle steamer also brought a reliable and regular transport system to the Highlands (Devine, 2006).

The estates in Strathconon were not unusual in following the trend of transfer to the new elite. Strathconon Estate itself was bought in 1839 by James Balfour (1773-1845) of Whittingham in East Lothian. He had made his fortune by supplying the British Navy with provisions whilst they were in Indian waters. Balfour not only amassed a sum of £300,000 by his enterprise but also married into the aristocracy; he had extensive estates in Fife and East Lothian. Scatwell Estate was more complicated. Meikle Scatwell had been bought by Mrs Stewart-Mackenzie of Seaforth in 1832 in an effort to consolidate her land in the east following the sale of her estates in the west. But in 1849 it was bought by Captain John Douglas and on his death in 1852 his wife added Little Scatwell. In 1853 Kinlochluichart and Glenmarksie had gone to William Bingham Baring, Lord Ashburton, son of the founder of Barings Bank. His wife Louisa, was the daughter of Mary Stewart-Mackenzie of Seaforth.

The new owners brought money with them. They undertook new building projects and new enterprises. Shooting lodges and houses were built, gardens landscaped and bridges erected. Sheep farming continued and was one of the main generators of revenue, but hunting, shooting and fishing also became important to the estate economics, and in addition played a part in providing employment for the population. The first reference to shooting on the Strathconon Estate, although only fragmentary, is in the 1820s when Lord O'Neil is described as taking a tack[1], possibly in Glen Meinich, for shooting. In the 1830s the Seaforth Trustees leased the Scardroy part of the estate for shooting. A lodge was built there c1836 and is described in the census records of 1881 as having 13 rooms. In the 1830s the interest was for shooting birds and fishing. An advertisement appeared in the *Inverness Courier* of 5 Aug, 1835

> The right of shooting and fishing over the upper district of Strathconon in Ross-shire is advertised to let. It is stated that grouse were most abundant and there were ptarmigan on several hills. The ground has been let for three years previously and its tenants asserted that it afforded excellent sport. One of them wrote that an ordinary shot might with great ease bag 20 brace of grouse in a day and he also said that he and one companion killed 13 brace of ptarmigan in about half an hour. A shooting lodge was in course of erection.

Balfour started to clear sheep from portions of his estate in order to make a deer forest in 1841 and following the clearances of 1850 the deer forest was extended; eventually,

---

[1] NAS GD46-17-59-00001

by the 1890s, it was to include the whole of the hill ground on the south side of the river from Dalbreac westwards. The deer forests were centred on Dalbreac and Scardroy, with Dalbreac being maintained for the use of the Balfour family, and Scardroy Lodge let to shooting tenants, although after 1854 it appears that Dalbreac too was let for tenants. Shooting rents were an important element of the estate income. In 1854 the Marquis of Bath was paying rent of £1200 for the estate, in 1868 John Shaw Leigh of Luton Hoo paid £1900 and in 1873 Hon RS Cotton paid £2,200; in total between 1853 and 1870 £50,446 was paid in rent for the shooting estate (Orr, 1891).

Dalbreac Lodge and its gardens were constructed in the early 1840s, on the south bank of the river and at the foot of a prominent wooded hill. The lodge was to have many additions and alterations, but in 1941 it was destroyed by fire. Low moss-covered stony mounds are all that remain today, but several ancillary buildings are used as estate offices or dwelling houses and some of the gardens and lawns are still maintained, but much is overgrown by rhododendrons. Three tees to the south of the buildings are the remnants of a six-hole golf course. Many of the stags heads, or trophies, which were on show in the "smoking room" of the lodge were rescued from the fire and now hang in the Community Hall.

James Balfour carried out building work in the vicinity of Dalbreac, Milton and Porin in the 1840s, following his purchase of the estate and before his death in 1845. Documents dated 1839 itemizing specifications[2] were found for the cottages at Bridgend. Later, James Maitland Balfour (1820-1856) continued with a spate of building construction and documents were found relating to a schoolhouse in 1848; for further building work at Scardroy Lodge and a barn and stables at Inverchoran in 1949; for a new meal mill and kiln at Milltown in 1851; for a blacksmith's house and office at Milltown and also for a keeper's house and dog kennels at Dalbreac in 1853. The 1853 plan[3] (*Fig. 39)* gives a good idea of the buildings in the area of Dalbreac, Milton, Porin and Dalnacroich at that time.

A keeper's lodge was constructed at Inverchoran and is still in use as such today. At Corriefeol a well appointed keeper's house has been occupied until relatively recently but is now roofless, the nearby byre has evidence of the pony stalls in its decaying plasterwork. A stone lined "mucking out" pit or midden and kennels are associated. In a ravine above Coirefeol there are the remains of an aerial ropeway probably used for transporting deer carcasses across the gorge. Throughout the Highlands stalker's paths provided access to the high mountains and are a feature of the deer forests. Their construction gave employment to many people and many paths are still in good order. A good example of a stalker's track leaves Corriefeol and makes its way around the hill into Coire Mhoraigein, it passes over a col at 550m, traverses a hillside in upper Glen Orrin and descends Gleann Chorainn to Inverchoran. Inverchoran Lodge has a sunken midden with a nicely cobbled floor similar to the one at Corriefeol.

Threshing mills with associated horse gangs or horse engines were found at two, possibly three locations in the glen - Corrievuic, Achlorachan and Mains of Dalbreac, but no documentary reference to the building of these mills was found. At Achlorachan the horse engine has the turning mechanism with its gearing still in place in the centre

[2] NAS GD433-3-3-6
[3] NAS RHP 2521

*Fig 55.* The keeper's pony byre at Corriefeol, with the stone lined midden in the foreground

of the horse walk. The horse would have walked in circles driving a shaft which passed, underground, into the adjacent building where it operated a threshing machine. At Corrievuic the horse gang and threshing barn seem out of place in a remote environment where it is difficult to imagine sufficient grain being grown to have made it worthwhile. At Dalbreac Mains Farm a tiny circle on the 1st Edition Ordnance Survey map next to the threshing barn provides possible evidence for a horse walkway. The adjacent threshing barn has a small rectangular aperture at head height indicating a possible entry point for an overhead shaft. The Balfours were almost certainly responsible for introducing these mills to Strathconon as they were known for being very progressive in their agricultural innovations on their East Lothian estates and it is probable that they brought some of their ideas north to Strathconon.

Arthur James Balfour (1848 - 1930) inherited the estate in 1856 on the death of his father James Maitland Balfour. Initially Arthur was a minor but he seems to have had an interest in his Strathconon estate at a later stage, until financial difficulty led him to let it out on a more permanent basis in 1885; in 1891 it was sold. In the latter part of the 19th century Arthur Balfour was to become a successful politician; he was Secretary of State for Scotland in the 1880s at the time of the Crofter's War, leader of the Conservative Party and Prime Minister of Great Britain from 1902 to 1903. Mr Gladstone stayed in Strathconon with his wife and daughter as a guest of Arthur Balfour on one occasion; he was very fond of the outdoor life and reluctant to leave when it came to the end of his visit. He was due in London for a cabinet meeting but put off his departure, sending his luggage the 16 miles to Muir of Ord and deciding to go overland the 5 miles to Achanalt to catch the train. He lingered until the last possible moment and then made a rough hurried journey over moor and loch

*Fig 56.* Recording the horse engine platform and mill at Achlorachan with plan below

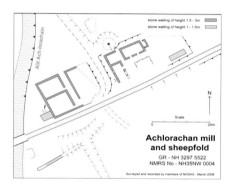

stone walling of height 1.5 - 3m
stone walling of height 1 - 1.5m

N

Scale
0                    25m

**Achlorachan mill
and sheepfold**

GR - NH 3297 5522
NMRS No - NH35NW 0004

Surveyed and recorded by members of NOSAS - March 2008

*Fig 57.* The central mechanism
of the horse engine

*Fig 58.* A horse engine in operation at Conisby, Islay, in 1981
© Royal Commission on Ancient and Historical Monuments of Scotland. Licensor www.scran.ac.uk

to Achanalt only just managing to make the train in time – Arthur Balfour got the blame![4]

RJ Combe bought the estate in 1891. Combe, Delafield and Co. was one of the major brewers in London in the 19th Century, but in 1898 was acquired by Watneys, becoming Watney, Combe and Reid. Captain Christian Combe inherited the estate and in about 1900 built the Community Hall at Milton; it is a fine example of its kind.

*Fig 59.* A postcard c.1930 of the Community Hall, left, and the old school, right.

Captain Combe and Lady Jane had two sons both of whom followed the family tradition of serving in the army. Colonel Henry Christian Seymour Combe, the elder of the sons, inherited the Stathconon Estate on the death of his father and the second son, John Fredrick Boyce, rose to the rank of General during the Second World War. The family's main residence was in Belgrave Square, London and Strathconon Estate continued in their possession until the 1950s when they sold the major part of it on the south side of the river, retaining the area in the upper glen which is now Scardroy Estate. This estate was sold in 1991 and soon after the old Scardroy Lodge was demolished and replaced by the present lodge built on the same site.

In 1849 the estate of Meikle Scatwell was bought by Captain John Douglas who built Scatwell House in 1850, adapting it, it is thought, from the old drovers inn built before 1800. John Douglas died in 1852 and his widow, Jemima, who continued at Scatwell House, extended the estate by purchasing the lands of Auchonachie, Cabaan in Glen Orrin (once part of Fairburn Estate), and Little Scatwell in 1853. For a time the two estates were united again and Mrs Douglas may well have built the shooting lodge over the hill at Cabaan. She certainly established a school at Scatwell, was responsible for the schoolmaster's salary and house and "made generous distribution of comforts to her

[4] NAS E433-2-85 Memoirs of Arthur James Balfour

tenantry". But in 1857 the two estates were split again when John Murray of Touchadam and Polmaise purchased Little Scatwell.

Perhaps the owner who left the most impression on Scatwell Estate over the latter part of the 19th Century was Dr William James Bell. He had possession of Scatwell House from 1864 to 1892. In 1890 he built a new wooden bridge, known as the Black Bridge, three kilometres down the river from Scatwell House. It provided the population with easier access to Contin and Strathpeffer, but it did not last long as it was washed away in a flood sometime after 1928. The abutments of this bridge are still to be seen and the timber piles are visible when the river is low. Dr Bell was responsible for introducing one of the earliest hydro electric schemes to the Highlands when he established a system of electric light for Scatwell House in 1889; more detail on this is given later in this chapter. Oral tradition has it that he may also have established a field telephone system, over the hill to Cabaan Lodge in Glen Orrin.

Sir James Buchanan and Lord Woolavington were owners of Scatwell from the 1890s to 1920s. They laid out the woodland and formal garden in their present form and were possibly responsible for the "model" farm which includes some fine farm buildings where a herd of pedigree dairy cattle was reared. In the 1930s Sir William Cross of the Coates Cross family, Paisley, was in possession and in the 1950s the family of Macdonald Buchanan, one member of whom married a daughter of Lord Woolavington, bought the estate.

Management of water has played a big part in the life of the people of the glen, as it almost certainly did in any rural community from early times. Several mill ponds and lades were identified during the project and in several instances it was evident that

*Fig 60.* The model dairy farm at Scatwell Farm

streams had been redirected and harnessed in order to drive waterwheels. Two were located in the vicinity of Scatwell House, one connected with the early township of Milltown of Scatwell, which had occupied the site prior to the building of Scatwell House and the other to provide power for an early sawmill. Nearby, Comrie has a substantial lade and mill pond but all traces of the mill have disappeared and in the central part of the glen, at Milton, there has probably been a mill for several centuries; the grain mill here survives and has been converted into a visitor centre, the slot for the water-wheel is still to be seen adjacent to the building. The complex system of lades, sluices and ponds at Milton has gone through a series of alterations and provided water for both a saw mill and a grain mill. In early times it was common for landlords to ban the grinding of corn by hand; instead they established mills and required that all their tenants should use them and pay the appropriate fees. One of the conditions of the multiple tenancy tacks of Strathconon given in 1803 reads[5]

It is hereby agreed that each one of the tenants before named shall grind all the grindable corn at the miln of Strathconon and pay the accustomed multures and miln dues for the same and perform the accustomed services thereat

*Fig 61.* The lade at Comrie

Two hydro-electric schemes were identified in the Scatwell area, both were interesting in that they were early examples of their kind in the Highlands. The earliest one was a private initiative to supply electric light to Scatwell House in 1889. Parts of this hydro-scheme are still to be seen on the hill to the south of the house, but it has mostly been replaced by a more recent scheme. The water is taken from the Allt a' Mhuillin which has been diverted to run into the Allt Dubh. The present pipe, with a cistern and valves, is on the line of the old one with the remains of the original generator shed buried in

[5] NAS RD2-293-00164

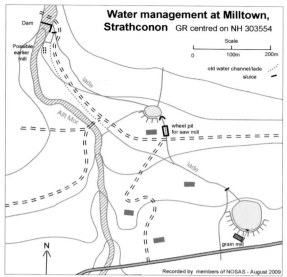

Fig 62. A plan of the complex system of lades, sluices and ponds for the mills at Milton

the rhododendrons to the north of the present shed. An article appeared in the *Scottish Highlander* on 10 Oct 1889

The Electric Light at Scatwell - Mr W.J.Bell of Scatwell has just introduced into his residence a system of electric lighting so complete and simple, that it will probably give an impetus to the extension of the new illuminant throughout the Northern Counties. The son of a leading scientist, Mr Bell possesses scientific tastes, and has always moved among scientific men, and probably the associations thus formed have induced him to take advantage of this invaluable means of illuminating a country residence. The arrangements are of the most simple character. In a little building about 200 yards from Scatwell House, the electricity is manufactured through the agency of a turbine wheel driven by water which comes from the hill above. From this spot, a pair of cables is carried to a chamber in the basement of the house, where, in a series of boxes or cells, the electric power is stored. In every room there is a knob like the handle of a bell; the turning of the knob in one direction sets up the electric communication and lights the room; the turning of it back severs the connection and extinguishes the light. The operation is, if possible, even more simple than the ringing of a parlour bell. For some of the rooms are also provided with portable lamps which can be connected by means of a short coil of cable with tubes in the wall. One convenient contrivance consists of a cigar light; a sort of ornament that hangs from the wall, and as it hangs has no connection with the electric wire. The mere act of lifting it up, however, forms the connection, and the lighted end is ready to communicate its spark to the cigar. In the principal bedrooms there are two handles for turning on the light; one at the door on entering, the other at the bedside. A person entering the room, or one lying in bed, can turn on and off the light at pleasure. There are in all eighty lights throughout the house.

The second hydro-scheme, at Conon Falls, was established in 1925 by the Ross-shire Electric Supply Company. Edward Blunt Mackenzie, the husband of the Countess of Cromarty, was the driving force behind the initiative. In 1903-04 he had developed a private enterprise to provide the communities of Strathpeffer and Dingwall with electric light through a scheme using water from Rogie, near Contin. The scheme however was costly and the company ran into debt and by 1925 Blunt Mackenzie, with bigger ideas and the assistance of a loan of £20,000, had built a dam across the River Conon with the aim of utilising the waters of Loch Luichart to feed two 500kw turbines. Ownership of the scheme passed to the Scottish Power Company in 1928 and the capacity of the Loch Luichart Power Station was increased again. By 1933 a transmission line was running up the Moray Firth seaboard from the generating station at Loch Luichart through Dingwall and the Easter Ross towns as far as Dornoch (Richards and Clough 1989).

Mica was a natural resource exploited in the glen on two occasions. Mica is heat resistant and when fashioned into thin slivers it was used for the "windows" of stoves and lamps. The remains of mica mines or quarries, the most recent of which date from the Second World War, are centred on NH 384 572, 500m to the northwest of Little Scatwell House. Twelve discrete quarry faces with their associated spoil heaps range over a steep spur in commercial woodland. The upper group of mines, or quarries, comprises six faces in close proximity to one another; they are much larger than the lower ones, some reaching a height of 10m and are believed to have been worked in the Second World War. On the lower side of the track, in the birch wood, there are the remains of a building which, because of its sunken nature, is thought to have been a store for explosives.

Timber has been an important resource in the glen and continues to be so today. In 1846 the woodland plantations of the "Black Wood" at Dalbreac and "Strathconan Wood" above Milltown, Porin and Dalnacroich were established as part of estate improvements. Both appear on the 1853 estate plan[6] and their extent is unchanged in 1872 when they are marked on the 1st Edition OS map. The 1st edition map also depicts natural woodland in many other parts of the glen, but by 1939-45 much of the woodland, both natural and planted, was being felled. Aerial photographs of 1947 give a good idea of the activities involved in the wartime felling; to the west and east of Inverchoran extensive tracts of barren hillside, timber camps and bridges are seen. Today, northeast of Inverchoran, little remains of the timber camp at the confluence of the Allt Gleadhrach and the River Meig apart from a few piles of stone and brick which were the Nissen huts. A brick chimney piece, now fallen, on the west side of the river next to the road is part of the same activity and a bridge, the abutment of which is still seen on the east bank of the river, at this same location is also related. Further west, at the outflow of Loch Beannacharain, there was another bridge and timber camp. Most of the commercial forests in the glen today were part of a large programme of planting in the 1950s and much of it is now in process of being felled.

[6] NAS RHP2521

# 13. The story of Finlay MacIver and his family

Finlay MacIver is not notable for any particular reason except that he and his family were typical of the many that lived in Strathconon at the time of the upheaval of improvement and conversion to sheep and deer. A study was made of his life events, in so far as the documents would allow, with the aim of discovering how he and his family fared in the longer term. His story reflects the lives of many in Strathconon, indeed of the Highlands. Finlay was chosen for 3 reasons; firstly because he was born and brought up in a part of the glen, Inverchoran to Invermeinie/Glenmeinie, which experienced dense population numbers and subsequent removal, secondly he was involved in distilling illicit whisky and lastly the name MacIver is not as common as many others in the glen, MacLennan, MacRae or Macdonald for example, and it was therefore easier to trace him in the documents. Having said that it was soon discovered that the surname MacIver was very prevalent in this particular area!

Finlay MacIver was born in 1804, most likely at Invermeinie/Glenmeinie, to Donald MacIver and his wife Flora whose maiden name was MacLennan. Donald MacIver's name appears as one of the multiple tenants at Invermeinie in the tack of 1803[1] where he is described as one of the former tenants. The tack of Invermeinie was given to nine tenants, three being resettled there following removal from West Balnault (on the south side of the river at Bridgend) to make way for the Dalbreac sheepfarm. They were Magdalen, Finlay and Duncan MacIver and it is possible that they were related to Finlay. In addition, the tack of neighbouring Carnoch was also given to three MacIvers, John, Duncan and Murdo, again possibly related. Finlay probably had several brothers and sisters but no mention of them was found in the Old Parish Records and it is probable that any births were not registered. Finlay married Margaret Macdonald on April 17th 1826, both were described as being "of Inverveinie". Margaret was born in 1802 and was the daughter of Donald Macdonald and his wife Christy, maiden name McDonald. Donald Macdonald does not appear in the 1803 tack of Invermeinie but three other Macdonalds do, so it is quite probable that he was related to them. It is clear that Finlay and Margaret had many relatives around them during their first 24 years of married life, and they would have seen many family members departing from the glen, particularly during the removals of the 1830s. Even so in the 1841 census there is still a significant number of MacIvers in the neighbourhood of Invermeinie, among them Flory MacIver, aged 70, probably Finlay's mother. The 1841 census lists 133 people in the area between Inverchoran and Crannich, today there are four. The names MacIver, MacLennan and Macdonald predominate and all are probably related to Finlay and Margaret in one way or another.

Finlay probably had no formal education as was the norm in the early 19th century. He was involved in the illicit distillation of whisky together with a Donald Mackay, possibly a brother-in-law, and Alexander Campbell, another relative. The court case was reported in the *Inverness Journal* on 29 April 1831.

Assault and deforcement of Revenue Officers - The diet was called against Alexander Campbell, otherwise McIvor, otherwise Broker, Finlay MacIvor or

[1] NAS RD2-293-00 p164-167

Broker and Donald Mackay all from Strathconnon. The two latter were outlawed for not appearing. The charge was that of having, on 14th May 1829 on the hill of Glenmeanie, deforced a party of Excise Officers and prevented them from continuing a survey which they had commenced in the district. Several persons connected with the Atlanta Revenue Cutter were examined for the prosecution who swore distinctly that the panel had along with others prevented the Revenue Officers from searching a bothy where they had reason to suppose illegal distillation was carried on, by rolling stones from he higher ground on the Excise Officers and their assistants and it appeared that the panel was one of the most active of the gang; he had called out several times to the officers "children of the Devil, if ye don't leave the glen we will have your lives". Neither Mr Cunningham, nor Mr Macdougal, Counsel for the Panel, addressed the jury. Lord Medwyn summed up the evidence shortly and the jury unanimously found the panel guilty upon which he was sentenced to 12 months imprisonment in the jail of Tain. Whether Finlay and his brother-in-law were caught and punished is not known.

Finlay and Margaret had seven children. Duncan born 1827, Donald 1830 and John 1834 were born at Inverveinie, Finlay 1838, Murdo 1843, Rory 1846 and Ann 1848[2] were born across the river at Crannich. In 1834 the family must have faced a dilemma when the tack of Invermeinie and Glen Meinich was taken over by John Fraser and a general reorganization of the tenancy followed. Many people were removed at this time and some settled on the Mulbuie Common on the Black Isle. Finlay and Margaret must have chosen to move to Crannich. The 1841 census has them there along with Donald McDonald, aged 35, and his family, possibly Margaret's brother. In 1849 the Strathconon school roll has Finlays sons Donald and Finlay registered, but no mention of John. John does not appear in any records after the 1841 census when he was age three and it is possible that he had died between 1841 and 1849 – child mortality was a common occurrence at this time and the circumstances of the potato famine, 1846 to 1850, must have contributed to malnutrition and disease resulting in an even greater number of child deaths

Finlay and Margaret would have witnessed the building of the Telford church in 1830 and the disruption of 1843 when many people left the established church to form the Free Church. They would have experienced the potato famine of 1846 and quite probably Finlay may have worked on the railways in the south or in the fields of the Black Isle. In 1847, following the potato famine, the family would have been given notice to quit their small farm under James Maitland Balfour's scheme of reorganization. The family may have been in arrears of rent but, at the age of 43, Finlay would have been considered fit to start a new life elsewhere and with four years notice may have been given work and the instruction in "good practices" offered by James Maitland Balfour and his factor, James Smith. All this would have stood him in good stead for his later move

Finlay and his family were part of a group of people who left Strathconon and settled at Knockfarrel, between Strathpeffer and Dingwall. They probably left Strathconon

---

[2] The births of Duncan, Donald and John are recorded in the Old Parish Records, the other children are on the 1841 census

before the termination of their lease at Crannich as a list of their names, which includes Finlay's, appears on a plan of the "Knockfarrail Allotments" produced in 1850. In 1848 John Hay Mackenzie, the Earl of Cromartie, had set about the reclamation of a considerable tract of boggy land at Knockfarrel but had died in 1849. His daughter Anne inherited the estate and married George Granville Sutherland-Leveson-Gower, Marquis of Stafford and later Duke of Sutherland. The improved land at Knockfarrel was sub-divided into lots and the evicted people of Strathconon were successful in petitioning Lady Stafford for the lots. In 1850 24 families were given 19 year leases of the plots (Richards and Clough 1989, p222-227).

The Knockfarrel settlers were reported as having accumulated considerable reserves of money in the bank "made by labour on the railways in the south" (Richards and Clough 1989, p229). Their settlement was called Gowertown in honour of Lord Stafford's family. The *Inverness Advertiser* reported on "the Strathconon Refuges" on August 6th, 1850

> these persecuted people are at present busily engaged with the assistance of some men from Dingwall in erecting cottages on lots kindly granted them by the Marchioness of Stafford at Knockferril. The lands which have been trenched about two years are also thoroughly drained and will, with unceasing labour, in course be pretty fertile. The ground is covered with a great many stones which will not be removed without much labour; and lime and manure which are absolutely necessary to its productiveness, cannot be conveyed thither owing to the roughness and steepness of the roads......We had the pleasure of a walk by this interesting place this week and of seeing the operations so energetically carried on by the Strathconon men. On both sides of this valley, and within short distances of each other, cottages are built. About 13 are already complete and occupied, and another three which are intended to be built will be erected in a few weeks. The houses are nice substantial buildings and contain a good deal of accommodation. The ground is divided into lots some 6, some 10 acres, and in some parts the soil is very fertile.

The task for Finlay must have been daunting, but he had the help of two of his sons. The 1851 census has Finlay's eldest son, Duncan, living with the family at Knockfarrel, presumably in order to assist his father. In the 1841 census Duncan, then aged 14, was working as an agricultural labourer at Scatwell. In 1851 Donald would have been 21 and it is quite likely that the younger sons, Finlay aged 13, and Murdo aged 8, would have been attending Fodderty School.

Finlay and Margaret's eldest sons seem to have done quite well for themselves. Duncan married Jane Mercer of Whittingham, near Haddington, in 1857. The marriage record describes Duncan as a forester of Dalbreck, Strathconon, and Jane as a housemaid, presumably they had met on one of the seasonal holidays when the Balfour family had brought their retinue from East Lothian north with them. In the 1871 census Duncan is described as a gardener living at the Gardener's House, Dalbreck, with Jane and their eight children; they continued there and by the 1891 census had 11 children. Donald married Isabella Urquhart in 1854 at the Anderston Institute in Elgin, he too is described as a gardener, but at Kinlochluichart Lodge. No records could be traced after this and it may be that the couple emigrated. There were no records either for Finlay's third son, Finlay, after 1851, but Murdo, Rory and Ann continue at Knockfarrel until at least 1871.

*Fig 63.* The improved croftlands of Knockfarrel today, with Dingwall and the Cromarty Firth beyond

Finlay's wife, Margaret, died in 1868, the register of deaths reports the cause as "fever for nine days" and on April 24th 1871 Finlay himself died of consumption (tuberculosis). The small holding at Knockfarrel continued in the hands of Finlay and Margaret's son, Murdo, and by this time the lands, originally worth 3/- an acre, were worth seven times as much.

It seems clear that the original people of the Knockfarrel "colony" remained closely knit as a group; they must have derived a good deal of support both physically and psychologically from each other during the years after 1850. Finlay's younger sons Rory (Roderick) and Murdo, married local girls, from Knockfarrel, in 1878. Roderick had made his way as a sheep farmer in Texas, America; he returned to marry Bella Mackay of Knockfarrel. She was the daughter of Duncan and Jessie Mackay who had been part of the group removed from Strathconon 28 years previously. Murdo married Christina, daughter of Donald and Jane Macdonald, also from the original Strathconon group. It may be assumed that Rory and Bella returned to America as they are not found in any of the censuses after their marriage. In the 1881 census Murdo, described as mason and crofter of 8 acres, and Christina, aged 27, are still at Knockfarrel with two children, Finlay 2 and Jane 1; by the 1901 census they have 15 children.

It would seem that the original people removed from Strathconon in 1850 had prospered. In 1883, William Gunn, factor of Cromartie Estate, reported to the Napier Commission (1884)

106

these people, with scarcely an exception, have proved to be excellent tenants in every respect. They are industrious and farm systematically and well and of this we have the best evidence in the fact that they pay their rents regularly and that within the last few years most of them have substantially improved their houses, four of which have lately been slated

In 1943, Colin Macdonald wrote of "the Cononachs" at Knockfarrel "they were the descendents of evicted forebears, who had industriously brought reclaimed land into cultivation, and were known for their friendliness and hospitable disposition." (Macdonald, 1943)

The people of the Knockfarrel "colony" were not too far from their roots in Strathconon, but they were a long way in terms of the poverty and the conditions which they had had to endure in the glen. Before 1850 many had had to cope with removal sometimes two and even three times, but at Knockfarrel they had had the security of long leases and been able to improve their land. They had also found themselves in an equally attractive place to Strathconon; Knockfarrel today is a favourite place for recreation. Finlay and Margaret had had to work hard to provide for themselves and their family, but they left a well established small holding for at least one of their sons when they passed on. They must have been happy that at least two of their sons had stayed in the area and done pretty well. It is quite possible that the other three sons emigrated, an option that was very much the norm for the Highlands in the second half of the 19th century. Perhaps they too found success and happiness on foreign shores.

# Bibliography

Anon, (1995, original version 1881) *Fearchair-a-Ghunna - The Ross-shire Wanderer*

Byam Shaw, Christina (Ed) (1988) *Pigeon Holes of Memory - The Life of Dr John Mackenzie*

Clough, Monica (1996) "Mackenzies of Scatwell" published in the *Clan Mackenzie Society Magazine*

Crawford, Barbara (1995) *Earl and Mormaer - Norse-Pictish relationships in Northern Scotland*

Cromartie, The Earl of (1979) *A Highland History*

Dagg, Catherine (2006) *Carnoch Church, Strathconon - Archaeological Investigation and Recording*

Devine, Tom (1988) *The Great Highland Famine*

Devine, Tom (1994) *Clanship to Crofters War*

Devine, Tom (2006) *Clearance and Improvement – Land, Power and People in Scotland, 1700-1900*

Dixon, J.H. (1886) *Gairloch*

Dodgshon, R. A. (1998) *From Chiefs to Landlords c1493-1820*

Downie, Rev. Charles (1837) *New Statistical Account for Contin Parish*

Fraser Mackintosh, C. (1898) "The Macdonald of Achtriachtan" in *Transactions of the Gaelic Society of Inverness, Vol XXIII*

Grant, A. (2000) "The Province of Ross and the Kingdom of Alba" in Cowan, E. and Macdonald R.A. (2000) *Alba, Celtic Scotland in the Middle Ages*

Hogg, James (1888) *Tour of the Highlands in 1803*

MacCoinnich, Aonghas (2009) "Strathconon, Scatwell and the Mackenzies in the written record, c1463-c1700" published by the North of Scotland Archaeological Society in Marshall, 2009

Macdonald, Colin (1943) *Highland Journey*

Macdonald, Iain S. (2005) *Glencoe and Beyond – The Sheepfarming Years 1780-1830*

MacInnes, Allan (1996) *Clanship, Commerce and the House of Stuart 1603 – 1788*

Mackenzie, Alexander (1879) *History of the Mackenzies*

Mackenzie, Alexander (1883) *History of the Highland Clearances*

Mackenzie, Osgood (1921) *A Hundred Years in the Highlands*

Mackenzie, Rev. Roderick (1791) *Old Statistical Account for Contin Parish*

McKichan, Finlay (2007) "Lord Seaforth and Highland Estate Management in the First Phase of Clearance (1783 – 1815)" in *Scottish Historical Review Vol LXXXVI*

McKillop, Andrew (2000) *More Fruitful than the Soil – Army, Empire and the Scottish Highlands 1715-1815*

MacLean, N. (1922) *The Life of James Cameron Lees*

MacLennan, Duncan (1996) *Strathconon*

MacPhail, J.R.N. (Ed) (1916) *Highland Papers Vol 2, Scottish History Society*

Marshall, M (2007) *Report of Phase 1 of a Project to Identify, Survey and Record Archaeological Remains in Strathconon, Ross-shire – Scatwell and Lower Strathconon*, by the North of Scotland Archaeological Society

Marshall, M (2008) *Report of Phase 2 of a Project to Identify, Survey and Record Archaeological Remains in Strathconon, Ross-shire Scardroy and Upper Strathconon,* by the North of Scotland Archaeological Society

Marshall, M (2009) *Report of Phase 3 of a Project to Identify, Survey and Record Archaeological Remains in Strathconon, Ross-shire - Loch Meig to Dalbreac,* by the North of Scotland Archaeological Society

Marshall, M (2010) *Report of Phase 4 of a Project to Identify, Survey and Record Archaeological Remains in Strathconon, Ross-shire – Strathanmore* to Loch Beannacharain, by the North of Scotland Archaeological Society

Miller, James (2002) *The Dam Builders*

Mowat, Ian R.M. (1981) *Easter Ross 1750-1850*

Munro, Jean and R.W. (Eds) (1986) *Acts of the Lords of the Isles 1336 – 1493*

Napier Commission (1884) *Evidence taken by Her Majesty's Commissioners of Inquiry into the condition of the Crofters and Cottars in the Highlands and Islands – Vol IV.*

Orr, W. (1991) *Deer Forests, Landlords and Crofters*

Richards, Eric (2000) *The Highland Clearances*

Richards, E. and Clough, M. (1989) *Cromartie, Highland Life 1650 – 1914*

Royal Commission (1892) *Report of the Royal Commission (Highlands and Islands, 1892) Vol 1* (Deer Commission)

Sage, Donald (1899) *Memorabilia Domestica*

Sinclair, Sir John (1795) *General View of the Agriculture of the North of Scotland*

Somers, Robert (1847) *Letters from the Highlands – after the Potato Famine of 1846*

Stewart of Garth (1829) "Observations on the Origin and Cause of Smuggling in the Highlands of Scotland" in the *Quarterly Journal of Agriculture 1829*

Watson, W.J. (1904) *Placenames of Ross and Cromarty*

Wordsworth, J. (2000) *Strathconon – An Archaeological Survey of several Woodland Grant Schemes*